THE EVERLASTING ARMS

THE EVERLASTING ARMS

The War Memoirs
of
Air Commodore
John Searby, DSO, DFC

Edited by

Martin Middlebrook

WILLIAM KIMBER · LONDON

First published in 1988 by
WILLIAM KIMBER & CO. LIMITED
100 Jermyn Street, London SW1Y 6EE

© Diana Searby, 1988
Editorial matter © Martin Middlebrook, 1988

ISBN 0-7183-0680-5

Photoset in North Wales by
Derek Doyle & Associates Mold, Clwyd
and printed in Great Britain by
Adlard and Son Limited,
Dorking, Surrey, and Letchworth, Hertfordshire

The Everlasting Arms

The title of this book is taken from a Chaplain's Prayer associated with the Royal Flying Corps, and often heard at Halton in my day.

Almighty God, who makest the clouds Thy chariot, and who walkest upon the wings of the storm; look down in mercy, we beseech Thee, upon all who are called to serve their country in the Royal Air Force. Help them to do their duty with prudence and fearlessness, confident that in life or death the Eternal God is their refuge, and underneath are the everlasting arms. Grant this for Jesus Christ His sake.

Amen.

Contents

List of Illustrations

Introduction

by

Martin Middlebrook

Air Commodore John Henry Searby, DSO, DFC, was a retired RAF officer with a distinguished wartime record who died in 1986, leaving the manuscript of a book describing that part of his wartime service which was spent in Bomber Command. He helped me with two of my own books and we were also jointly involved in a television programme and several other events. I am proud of this association and of his friendship; to me he was 'John' and I am certain that he would not have objected at my reference to him as 'John Searby' in this introduction and in the editorial notes added to his book.

John Searby was born on 23rd April 1913 at Whittlesey, near Peterborough. His birth certificate describes his father as a journeyman-wheelwright; John inherited his father's skill and spent many hours in his own workshop. His paternal grandparents were from north Lincolnshire, his mother's family came from the Spalding-Peterborough area. John hardly knew his father because he volunteered for the Army and, as Sapper J.W. Searby, 202nd Field Company, Royal Engineers, was killed in the Battle of the Somme on 11 October 1916 (his grave is in Caterpillar Valley Cemetery, Longueval). This was the second loss by the Searby family in the Battle of the Somme; John's Uncle Fred had been killed with the 1st Lincolnshires at Fricourt in July 1916. John and his mother were living at or near the grandparents' home in the village of Withern, near Louth, when the two Searby brothers were killed and John once told me of his admiration for his grandparents' quiet fortitude at the loss of two sons and how their attitude affected his own development. After the war, John's mother moved to Spalding and John spent his schooldays there, being known to his schoolfriends as 'Harry' (in the RAF he became 'John' again and, on at least one squadron, was known as 'Honest John').

At the age of sixteen, while at Spalding Grammar School, John won a scholarship after a written examination and was awarded a place in the Aircraft Apprentices Scheme at RAF Halton in Buckinghamshire. This excellent scheme was started in 1920 by Lord Trenchard, not only to provide the RAF with trained technicians but also to create a pool of men who might be suitable for future aircrew training. The establishment of the scheme at that time resulted in the 'Halton Brats', as they are often called, constituting a large proportion of the RAF's pilots and other aircrew on the outbreak of war in 1939. It was an excellent means by which clever and hardworking boys from modest backgrounds could progress through to aircrew status and eventually to commissioned rank.

Competition for entry to Halton was intense, with up to ten applicants for each place. Once accepted, the apprentice spent three years on general and technical training, gradually being directed to the trade for which he was most suited; John Searby became a 'Fitter (Aero-engine)'. The pay was one shilling per day (three shillings per week payable during term time and four shillings per week held back until end-of-term leave). Those apprentices successfully completing the three-year course were allocated ranks depending on their examination results. The top twenty per cent became Leading Aircraftmen, the next 20 per cent Aircraftmen 1st Class and the remainder Aircraftmen 2nd Class; John Searby managed to attain the second grade and thus became AC1 Searby, with a daily pay of 4/3d (about 21 pence in to-day's currency) and a commitment to stay in the RAF for twelve more years.

On leaving Halton, his service certificate also carried the notation that he was 'considered suitable for future employment as an airman pilot' and two years later, in 1931, he was posted to a Flying Training School at Grantham, graduating as a Sergeant Pilot with a 'Distinguished Pass'. Not much is known of the next few years (because his log book was later lost) but he served with three bomber squadrons – 104, 106 and 108 – and he was commissioned late in 1939, the year in which he married Eva Rowland, whose father had also been killed in the First World War, coincidentally also in the Battle of the Somme (in the East Surreys) and, like John's father, also near the village of Longueval.

There were five children of John's marriage, two sons and three daughters. One son eventually became an Army officer in a famous cavalry regiment; one daughter became a WAAF officer and then married an RAF officer.

So John Searby entered a second war, one of that body of aircrew who would carry the traditions of the old RAF into a vastly expanded wartime force. This dwindling band of professionals were the men who provided early inspiration and later the leadership of operational squadrons in the middle years of the war. The end of the war would find the few survivors in command or staff positions, prisoner-of-war camps or as cripples. John Searby's memoirs contain a long catalogue of peacetime friends lost on operations, nearly all being killed.

But John Searby's squadron – 108 at Bassingbourn, flying Blenheims – did not immediately go to war, being one of those squadrons withdrawn from the front-line for reserve and training purposes. He was soon posted to the long Specialist Navigation Course in Canada, and later to a Blenheim Operational Training Unit in England as an instructor. His next move was to Ferry Command, where he helped to open up the Atlantic Ferry, flying Hudsons from Newfoundland to Scotland or from Brazil to Africa. It was not until October 1941 that he was able to return to more warlike operations when he flew two familiarization operations with a Canadian bomber squadron in October and November 1941, these probably not being obligatory flights but flights made at his own insistence before being posted to an operational squadron. He still had to wait nearly a further year before being posted as a flight commander to 106 Squadron at Syerston and commencing regular operations. His book describes the next year in great detail, including periods in successful command of two squadrons, a good example of the farsightedness of Trenchard's Halton Apprentice Scheme. His operational career spanned an interesting time, seeing the early operations of the Lancaster, the development of the Pathfinder Force of which he became a member, rapid changes in tactics, the successes of the Battles of the Ruhr and Hamburg. As flight and squadron commander, he was at the top levels of the operational body of aircrew, much aware of the decisions being taken by commanders and of the clashes of personalities of those commanders but, on his part, bearing the heavy responsibility of dispatching hundreds of young men on operations.

John Searby survived, with the rank of Acting Group Captain and with the DSO and DFC. He was the only one or four consecutive commanding officers of 83 Squadron not to be shot down and killed. The period from which he emerged saw the climax of his operational career and a place in history when he acted as Master Bomber on the Peenemünde Raid, the first time an officer attempted to control the whole of Bomber Command over a target; the method he introduced that night to destroy the German V-2 rocket establishment at Peenemünde was adopted on many later raids and added substantially to the effectiveness of the bomber campaign.

After a period of rest from operations (though not from duty) he might well have been called back for a tour as a station commander, with the need to fly further operations, but his 'Specialist Navigation' qualification took him to a safe but useful job at Bomber Command Headquarters. This period, to me, was one of the most interesting parts of the book, because he covers an aspect of Bomber Command rarely written about. He describes the tension and the pressure connected with the mounting of daily bomber operations and some of the infighting which took place at that high level. He also describes the extreme firmness and remoteness of Sir Arthur Harris's style of command.

John Searby remained in the RAF for a further sixteen years. He saw service in Transport Command, at Headquarters Mediterranean and Middle East Air Force, as OC of the Flying Wing at Manby Flying College, had postings to Canada and to the United States, completed various staff college courses, and finally returned to Bomber Command Headquarters as Director of Bomber Operations, Missiles and Reconnaissance. He retired prematurely from the Royal Air Force for personal reasons in 1961. In the following years he devoted much time to research, writing and the production of tapes describing wartime raids and at his workbench. He died of a heart attack in his office-cum-workshop at Brandon in Norfolk on 14th January 1986.

Martin Middlebrook, September 1987.

Editor's Acknowledgements

Mrs Emmie Bolton, John Searby's mother-in-law of his first marriage; Chris Everitt, who carried out research at the Public Record Office and at Halton; Ron Low, historian of 83 Squadron; Air Commodore Joe Northrop, DSO, DFC, AFC, on the same course as John Searby at Halton and at one time one of his flight commanders on 83 Squadron; Des Richards, historian of 106 Squadron; Squadron Leader Norman Scrivener, DSO, DFC, John Searby's wartime navigator; Mrs Diana Searby, John's second wife; the Air Historical Branch (MOD); the Commonwealth War Graves Commission.

Prologue

The hill seemed steeper than I remembered it. I climbed slowly,
following the chalk path to the crest and found that for which I
was looking – a small clearing, still recognisable, though the trees
were taller than they used to be. Thankfully, I sat down with my
back against a fine beech, a mature and very handsome specimen,
thickly leaved, affording a welcome shade from the heat of the
sun. Time did not matter; nothing moved and the silence was
heavy. Looking out over the great camp I detected few changes
though the old station headquarters had gone and a new building
stood in its place, fronting the carefully mown lawn on which the
massed pipe bands and kettledrums used to beat 'Retreat'. Right
and left the long spur of the Chiltern Hills was visible, and at its
foot the old road – the Icknield Way – ran on down to Wendover
as it had always done. I felt content; the climb had been
worthwhile, and I closed my eyes for a moment ...

'It's been a long time' – I heard a voice from nearby.

'Not all that long,' I replied, 'and I'm here now.'

'I should think so, after all these years. Why haven't you come to
see us before?'

'Oh, I've been busy. Many things to do and many
responsibilities. Yes, I have been fully occupied.'

'Have you? I must say you carry them easily. Were they very
onerous ... because you don't look very different?'

'Indeed they were, as you say, onerous.'

'So, you didn't come back?'

'No – this is my first visit after very many years ... and I've
changed a lot. We all do, you know.'

'You think so? *We* don't see any change.'

'I'm much older for one thing.'

'But are you any wiser?'

'Certainly – I know so much more about life.'

'And has this knowledge made you any happier?'

'That is an awkward question – you shouldn't ask it.'

'Don't mind me – I'm a very old friend, and old friends may speak their minds.'

'I suppose so … and the answer is "Yes and No".'

'Did you become Chief of the Air Staff – that *was* your ambition I seem to recall.'

'Er … no, … I missed that one.'

'But you became an Air Marshal, surely? We had great hopes for you.'

'I'm afraid I didn't – not my fault. There were many fellows to choose from.'

'A pity – what went wrong?'

'Nothing, really – I did all right – luck of the draw, you know.'

'You remember Geoffrey?'

'Of course – how could I forget him?'

'He was your best friend and you swore eternal friendship. Have you seen him since you left us?'

'No – and I'm sorry … I meant to write … he did write to me you know?'

'Yes, we know. He came back here to see us one day.'

'Did he? I wish I had written. He was a great chap.'

'Too late now, I'm afraid.'

'I can't forgive myself. Did he ask about me?'

'Indeed he did – but we had nothing to tell him.'

'I'll come again – will you be here?'

'We are always here – surely you know that? So, you will come again?'

'I promise.'

'Goodbye.'

'Goodbye.'

*

The sun was lowering and the air cool. I got up and made my way back down the hill past the empty-barrack blocks of No 4 Wing which had once housed a thousand apprentices. The Wing HQs was shut up, and the great gun, a piece of World War One artillery, was no longer in place. Only the parade ground which my poor old feet had pounded so heartily for three long years, was unchanged. Here, the Wing Sergeant Major stood on his stool and bawled at us as we performed the elaborate drill movements of that day: 'Pull on those butts – your rifle is not neck-tie – swing your arms shoulder high' (I could never see the sense in that).

Smartness, precision, and no wonder; the bulk of the senior NCOs had been recruited from the Brigade of Guards, especially to lick the infant Royal Air Force into shape. Breeches and puttees – tunics tight at the neck – oh, we were very proud of our uniforms – dress was all important and image had to be good since we carried with us more than just the trappings of the RAF, then eleven years old ... the stalwarts of the Royal Flying Corps stood behind us. We had been entrusted with a tradition, won in a few short years and never to be forgotten. In the lecture rooms and laboratories where theory was taught they looked down at us – Ball, McCudden, Mannock and the rest; in their reflected glory we strove mightily. Three shillings a week for the first year and five after that with an increment put aside for leave. How wise a policy – I went home once with six pounds in my pocket – a small fortune.

Life was tough and life was earnest. There existed a great gulf between the wing with its harsh discipline and the workshop school complex. In the latter, lay all that I had joined for and which compensated for the fierce drill sergeants and the snapping corporals up at the wing. Theory of flight, theory of heat engines, metallurgy, dynamics, hydraulics – technical drawing and machine tools. Nothing slip-shod – all work as near perfection as the hand can guide; the limits were tight and, if you didn't get it right the first time round, then begin again. The ex-naval engine room artificers who taught in the workshops were firm and not without humour – in stark contrast to the Guards drill instructors up in the wing. My guru was an ex-Chief ERA who had been blown out of his engine room at Jutland and somehow survived: his stories of the Grand Fleet which ruled the waves up to World War One had us holding our sides with laughter – there was plenty of goodwill among the Navy men and they commanded enormous respect. Steam was their element – nothing could match steam – and all good engineers came up that way!

And sport ... the fit man did things better: all doors were open to the *victor ludorum*. The opportunities were many and there was plenty of encouragement, boxing, running, the passage-at-arms with foil, *épée* and sabre – even golf on the tricky course at the top of the hill. Church parade took place every Sunday and three wings of apprentices crammed into the converted workshop under the eyes of the wing and squadron commanders, hugely decorated with the DSOs and DFCs gained a few years earlier.

Officers and gentlemen, their emblems of gallantry tinkled on their uniformed chests, to our great delight.

Never complain, never explain – not a bad rule. A lie may be forgiven if it will save a friend, though not all will agree. When the chips are down and the going is rough – hold on; others are copping it worse than you. If you can't discipline yourself then don't expect to discipline the men entrusted to you. The man who sticks at the controls long enough to get his crew clear of the blazing bomber, regardless of his own safety, (and that was the fate of many) follows a tradition created by the Royal Flying Corps; a thousand trumpets will see him over the last hurdles. When I left Halton I had another three months to go to my nineteenth birthday, and seven years were to elapse before our manhood would be tested. My friend Geoffrey, with whom I climbed the hill in carefree days, and to whose dreams and ambitions I had been partner, did not survive the conflict.

CHAPTER ONE

'The smell of cordite'

The Lancaster settled into the bombing run. The smell of cordite was strong; the German gunners were pumping the stuff into the calculated point of release of the bombs, where the laws of probability operated with a neat precision. A few could cop it here, not many, but enough to jutsify the expenditure of so many shells. The searchlight cones were more deadly; the blue master beam locked on and instantly a dozen others grouped closely round it imprisoning the huge bomber – and up came the iron – salvoes of high explosive – with the razor-edged lumps of cast steel ripping into the victim. The flatter the cone the more difficult to escape its embrace. I heard the cool voice of the bomb aimer:

'Left a bit – left – hold her there' and the seconds ticked by:

'Bomb doors open.'

Automatically my left hand sought the lever and the big doors swung open exposing the 'cookie' and the incendiaries. This was the moment of truth, concentrating the mind wonderfully ... the barrage was intense and the searchlights stripped us naked, then, a rumble beneath my feet,

'Bombs gone, skipper.'

The ordeal was half over; we yet must remain straight and level for the camera to record the impact. The little red light in the dash came on; until it went out we were committed and it would burn until the bombs struck. The seconds ticked by and the perspiration was trickling down my face – thirty more before that little lot reached the ground – an eternity it seemed – but the end came and we were free. I swung the nose up and she rose like a bird to climb away from the sickening crunch of the heavy flak and the cold white fingers of the searchlights. I saw one of our number sustain a direct hit – for a few seconds he hung, a blazing mass, between the silent stars and the tumult below – to disintegrate into thousands of burning fragments. Mission accomplished, empty chairs in the mess on the morrow.

The short run back to the Dutch coast was accomplished without incident and we landed back on the home airfield after five hours in the air. A Ruhr sortie, nothing special.

Casualties had been light; fourteen aircraft missing from a total of 440 dispatched – for a Ruhr attack – and Bomber Command could sustain losses of around three percent. The remarkable thing about this operation was the extreme accuracy of the Pathfinder marking: nothing like this had occurred in the long history of 'Ruhr-bashing' and it boded well for the future. At this time I was nearing the endy of my current tour of operational duty, serving as 'B' Flight Commander since the previous October and, though I did not know it, I was to succeed Guy Gibson as squadron commander in ten days' time.

When I joined No 5 Bomber Group some six months earlier, the Lancaster was making its debut. The aircraft had surpassed all expectations in range, speed and bomb capacity, though as yet production was slow, and sufficient only to equip a single bomber group under the command of Air Vice-Marshal Alec Coryton. Competition was keen where squadron and flight commander posts were involved and all prospective candidates were interviewed by the AOC. My own background was not remarkable. I had made a number of crossings of the Atlantic as a ferry pilot and among bomber men of that era that was very small stuff. However, I got the job. Alec Coryton was a splendid man – the archetype of senior officer – being shrewd, able and well informed; and a bit autocratic. He ranked with Air Vice-Marshals Roddy Carr and Sir John Baldwin – all 'greats' and much respected.

The interview was short yet brisk: 'I want my aircraft flown to the limit and I expect flight commanders to set an example.' He asked few questions; his manner was quiet and his address courteous. I went on my way and, after a fortnight at the Conversion Unit, I set out for Syerston to join No 106 Squadron commanded by Wing Commander Guy Gibson, DFC and Bar.

Syerston lies on the Fosse Way between Newark and Nottingham. On that warm October afternoon, the tall elms cast long shadows across the road, and the omens seemed good. The choice was mine; no one had pressed me to launch into the business of bombing Germany and I had left a very comfortable staff appointment behind me. Sooner or later the Personnel Department would have caught up with me, no doubt, but it wasn't that which motivated me. It was fear – fear of being left out, fear of being in the company of men who had fought the war and with nothing to show for my own endeavours. On the North Atlantic I had no such fear – there were few aids to help one in those days; the satisfaction of putting her down on the Prestwick runway after a bad weather crossing was real enough. Twelve hours on the Great Circle from Newfoundland to Scotland in a twin-engined Hudson with just sufficient petrol to make it was always a challenge but, as Guy Gibson was to say to me the following morning, 'You can forget all that; it means nothing. This is the real thing.' He was contemptuous of anything outside his own world of striking down the enemy.

Apart from an acute shortage of furniture the mess was very comfortable, being a permanent building not long completed. There was a bed in my room and an old card table and it was only afterwards I understood the significance of his words. Furniture moved from room to room in direct ratio to the casualty rate in both squadrons! I did not have to wait more than a day or two before I was equipped with both a wardrobe and a fine chest of drawers!

Charlie Hill – squadron leader commanding 'A' Flight – was an old friend from the Blenheim days and, like myself, a recent arrival. He occupied a room on the other side of the passage and I tapped on his door to receive a warm welcome. He was pulling on his flying boots.

'We're on tonight, John. Glad to have you with us. I'll take you round the place in the morning.' Charlie was a very sound officer with a good 'ops' record in 2 Group, the light bomber group, where he had won a DFC, and I expressed surprise at his translation to the heavy brigade.

'It's OK – one aeroplane is very much like another. My number came up for a second tour and there were no vacancies going in the Mosquito squadrons so I took this.'

'How do you get along with Gibson?'

'All right – as long as you're willing to fly over Germany he's happy. We badly need another flight commander to share the work and you've come at the right moment.'

The Tannoy blared its message: 'All crews report to Flights.'

'Where is it tonight, Charlie?'

'Cologne.' He was about to leave. 'Perhaps you'll keep an eye on her for me? She gets a bit restive when I'm away – she likes company.' The small black spaniel in the basket got up and walked over to me, 'You see – she understands what I say. All right, old girl, I shan't be long.' He patted the animal and left for the airfield. I finished my unpacking and went up to Flying Control in time to see the take-off.

The airfield lay in total darkness save for the blue lights set either side of the perimeter track along which the slow moving bombers proceeded in close column to the runway threshold. At half minute intervals they roared off displaying a momentary flash of wing-tip and tail lights as they sped down the long east-west runway to disappear in the night. The thunder of the Merlin engines died away; it would be another five hours before the airfield came to life again.

I walked across to Squadron Headquarters, one of the familiar Laing huts, and noted the names on the various doors – Gunnery Leader, Navigation Officer, Bombing Leader, Signals Section – and I paused at the offices used by the two flight commanders, one bearing Charlie Hill's name and the other bare. This would be mine on the morrow. Inside I found a battered table sporting a grubby blotting pad covered with doodles and telephone numbers: the chair had a broken spell and the door of the steel clothing locker hung open to reveal a blue woollen scarf and a grimy pair of tennis shoes. Leaning against the wall was a large sheet of perspex set out with the names of the crews and the letters of their aircraft. An official poster hung on the wall showing a glamorous WAAF seated on the tail of a Spitfire and the caption read 'Fly with Prudence'. Curiously, something of the personality of my predecessor remained – I felt it strongly, or fancied I did so – and I knew that the record of the squadron, in terms of casualties among its flight commanders, was not a happy one.

Back in the mess I found a pencilled note lying on the card table which read as follows: 'Sir, I hope you find everything you need sorry about no wardrobe and such and will bring your tea at 0645 sharp.' It was signed 'Your batman'. My kit had been laid out on a sheet of brown paper – in the absence of a chest of drawers – and he had done a neat job, folding things and stacking them in rows. Since the squadrons would not return for some hours I decided to get my head down for a while. Around midnight I intended to go back to see them in and possibly meet Gibson in the interrogation room. I was short on sleep, having flown most of the previous night completing my course on the Lancaster at the Conversion Unit. That done, no time had been lost in sending me on my way to Syerston though I heartily welcomed the move; Henry Maudsley and Rupert Oakley were excellent instructors – none better – but I found the atmosphere too restrictive for my taste.

The best thing that happened to me at the Conversion Unit was the acquisition of a first class flight engineer – an Australian, Frank Forster, who stayed with me for many long months and later elected to accompany me to the Pathfinder Force. He was a volunteer all the way from Sydney and I sometimes wondered what induced him to leave home and travel half across the world to fly with Bomber Command. He never told me.

I awoke around ten o'clock. A dog was whining and I got up and went into Hill's room where the spaniel was fretting so I carried her back with me and endeavoured to settle her down. After an interval she began whining steadily but I dozed off once more only to wake up and find it was two o'clock in the morning. I had overslept and the squadron had already landed. The spaniel was scratching at the door of my room and obviously trying to get to her master – but his room was empty. Pulling on some clothing I picked her up and made my way to the main ante room where a solitary officer sat by the embers of a dying fire. It was Martin, the squadron adjutant, and he rose to take the dog from me, saying:

'All right, sir; I'll look after her; she won't be seeing her master again. We've had a bad night – three Lancasters missing, including Squadron Leader Hill; the other two were among the best we had and near the end of their tours of duty.'

I went back to my room and fetched the basket: the animal *knew* and had first started whining about the time Hill had been shot down! There is no explaining these things.[1]

With Hill missing, I was the only remaining flight commander – and as yet I had not even started on the job. I slept uneasily and was awakened by a brisk young Irishman with a cup of tea:

'Good morning, sor. I'm O'Brien, your batman. An unlucky night for the squadron, sor – Squadron Leader Hill is missing and him not long with us – I'll get his wardrobe for you later on. Such a foine man, sor – very quiet he was and we shall miss him.' His calm acceptance of events depressed me: there was nothing unusual about this kind of situation and Hill was the third flight commander to go missing in a very short space of time.

Later that day I reported to the squadron commander – Wing Commander Guy Gibson, DFC and Bar. It was an extraordinary meeting. He had been flying the previous night and was under some strain. He asked me what I had been doing before joining him – and heard me out with obvious distaste – impatient and barely polite. He was a small man – with a fresh complexion, and I thought, cocky as they come. I was brief but he cut in:

'You can forget all that – it means nothing. Anything you may have done before you came here is nothing. *This is the real thing.*' He got up from his desk and walked to the window, hands thrust deeply into the pockets of his uniform jacket. Then, 'Ops are what count here – and anyone who doesn't like it can get out.'

I began to dislike him, but sensed this was a bad moment; the letters to the next of kin of the men who were missing lay on his desk awaiting signature – three Lancasters and their precious crews was a nasty knock.

Once again: 'Forget it – it means nothing.'

I saluted and left the office; there was no more to be said – no time for trivia – no welcome but the blunt truth – and his unspoken words amounted to this – 'You are a general duties officer – Flying Branch – so, bloody well fly and prove it.'

These were very early days and I think he was right both in what he said and in his attitude. We understood each other from the word go and we had our differences, not infrequently, and though storms blew up he could forget them in a day. He was a supreme leader of men in war – and in no wise would he set a task he could not perform himself and do better than anyone else.

When I walked into 'B' Flight Office it was occupied. A fair-haired flight lieutenant sat in the chair with his feet on the table, very much at ease. He did me the courtesy of getting to his feet.

'Good morning, sir. I'm Hopgood, deputy flight commander.' He was cool and faintly whimsical – as if he found it hard to take me seriously.

'Hoppy', as he was known throughout No 5 Group, was a veteran bomber captain; one of a fast diminishing band, typical of his class and background, being an excellent pilot, brave, experienced and essentially a squadron 'type'. He had proved himself over and again in battle and attacked every major target in Germany. Tall, with an easy manner, he could lead in both the air and on the ground; especially in short range forays to nearby hostelries where the fun was innocent and, occasionally, furious. Gibson liked and trusted him; he was among the first to be chosen when the Dams Squadron was formed in the spring of 1943 and he lost his life at the Möhne Dam. On this, my first morning, he kindly took me round the dispersal area and similar places; we viewed the battle damage to the Lancasters after the Cologne raid and I met the ground staffs.

At lunchtime when I returned to my room I found it completely furnished. I had acquired most of Hill's furniture which had been pushed across the corridor and the much prized wardrobe stood in the corner. Poor Charlie, his time had been short ... and how long might it be before the wardrobe made another move along the corridor? The question came unbidden and was quickly dismissed.

Since a 'stand-down' had been decreed, I returned to the office and put my feet up on the table as Hoppy had done. I deeply regretted Charlie's going but there was no sense in dwelling on it; the best thing was to get on with the job. I had plenty of good flying experience behind me excluding the Atlantic Ferry and, though I appreciated the difference between that and operating over Germany, I had a notion that the experience would prove useful, as indeed it did. It was a little more than a year since I completed my last delivery of a Hudson aircraft – picked up at Montreal and flown by night over the North Atlantic to Prestwick – and during the summer of 1941 I had done a similar job flying between Florida and West Africa. Over the great oceans the only enemy was the weather and, occasionally, fatigue: here the weather would still be a factor but the other enemy was more deadly still. I was not entirely ignorant of his methods since I had flown a few operations in Wellingtons – for experience only, and designed to help in the newly created drive for more accurate navigation on the part of the bomber crews – but these sporadic sorties were far removed from the steady day to day routine of the officers and NCOs who manned the front line squadrons and I never mentioned them to Gibson. In this context it might be as well to recount my experience with the Canadians – No 405 (RCAF) Squadron – a rough and ready bunch of individuals but warm and friendly from the moment I arrived on temporary attachment from Bomber Command Headquarters.

'The man's crazy – he wants to fly with us!' said one.

'OK, put him in the programme for Hamburg – that'll cool him down,' said another.

They did, and after the briefing I joined them at the long table in the mess dining room where I was made welcome: no frills but plenty of leg-pulling. They had some good officers and every man was a volunteer for service overseas. I knew no one present but it wasn't important and I had barely got stuck into my bacon and eggs when a loud voice boomed at me from the far end:

'Say, you're new here, aren't you?' I said I was. The large Canadian grinned: 'And you're on the programme tonight, eh?' I nodded – yes, I was going to Hamburg with one of the crews. There was a pause, then he came in again: 'Tell me, bud – what size is your greatcoat?'

Roars of laughter from the assembled crews – at my expense. This particular squadron had taken a beating over the past weeks and I did not miss the point. The man on my right was also interested,

'You're not just going for the ride, are you?'

'No,' I replied, 'I hope to take some star shots.'

This remark created a certain amount of interest. 'But you are a pilot,' he said. 'How come?'

'That's right – I am also a navigator, it's simple.'

There was silence for a moment then I heard, 'The guy's nuts – but I guess he knows his business.' After that I was in.

It proved a hit and miss affair. We didn't find Hamburg – Hamburg found us. From a point just south of Heligoland we altered course for the mouth of the Elbe where the weather became very thick and nasty with embedded cu-nims, thunderous, and loaded with freezing rain, thumping and tearing at the old Wellington. Up front our pilot, a sturdy young NCO named Williams, pressed on doggedly, easing her through the worst of the up-currents whilst concentrating on his instrument panel. Over what I calculated to be Cuxhaven we were greeted with a flurry of heavy ack-ack shells accurate for height but wide of the aircraft. There was no question of finding a helpful pinpoint in that blackness and by dead reckoning we had only a few minutes to go to the target when quite suddenly the sky erupted all around us – we flew in a welter of bursting cordite and the noise was fantastic.

'Captain to navigator, we are over Hamburg – get 'em off quick – I'm not hanging around in this lot.'

The navigator queried this statement, 'We're not there yet, skipper – another two minutes to go to ETA.' A salvo of six well-aimed shells seemed to ring the Wellington at this moment and the harassed pilot was in no mood to argue,

'Never mind the bloody ETA – dump the lot – fast – I'm getting out.'

No bomb aimer was carried in the Wellingtons and the navigator quickly jettisoned his load; in the circumstances, and with no hope of seeing the ground, it was the right treatment. Then, unhampered by a heavy bomb load, our stout captain treated us to the most astonishing display of aerobatics – diving her until the airspeed indicator registered 280 mph and pulling up the nose until she was at the point of stall – and all the time we were in thick cloud with ice particles lashing the windows and the airframe groaning at the unwelcome stresses induced by the savage manoeuvres.

We got clear eventually and made our way back across the North Sea to Yorkshire sick and weary – and certainly chilled to the bone with the biting cold. We never saw the heavens from start to finish and when we met the others in the Interrogation Room I was reminded of our conversation over supper: 'Well, how many of them star shots did you get on that trip, friend – I guess it was not your night.'[2]

I flew with 405 Squadron on several occasions but this attachment is more memorable for the events of 7th November 1941 than anything else. This was the night when attacks were made on a number of targets and some 37 bombers were lost. Considering the total strength of the Command was no more than 500 of all types at this stage of the war a loss of this magnitude created alarm – and there were questions asked. Of the 400 bombers dispatched that evening 169 went to the 'Big City' – which claimed 21 crews whilst the other sixteen were lost over Mannheim, Cologne and less important targets. It was a night of foul weather out over the North Sea and the weather forecast spoke of very strong headwinds for the return. I attended the briefing and, in common with most of the Canadian crews I expected a cancellation – but it didn't happen.

Each Wellington of 405 Squadron carried a 4,000 lb bomb and at that loading the maximum range was 1,400 statute miles. Berlin lies some 600 miles from the Yorkshire bomber bases; thus under normal conditions a safety margin of one hour was available. Well, these were not average or normal conditions and here lay the cause I believe, of most of the losses. Squadron Leader John Fauquier, as he then was, commanded one of the flights in 405 and was none too happy about the weather forecast we both heard that evening. This is what he wrote to me years later,

On the night of 7/8 November 1941 the squadron was called to briefing when we were told our target was to be Berlin. When it was time for the Met boys to predict our weather I immediately smelt a rat, as they were very nervous and seemed unable to make up their minds what the wind velocity would be for the return trip. All went well on the outward bound flight until we climbed out of the overcast, after which we were on dead reckoning ... When we reached a point where we believed, and hoped, Berlin was we dropped our bombs and turned for home. It didn't take long before we realised we were in trouble, as the winds had increased. As soon as it was safe to do so I dropped down to sea level for two reasons. Firstly, to avoid ice and thus save fuel and secondly I hoped we might experience a little less headwind.

I have seen the North Sea in many moods, but I have never seen it in a more ferocious mood before or since that night. Huge waves of solid green water were being lifted out of the sea and carried hundreds of feet by the wind. After what seemed like hours ... I realised we were going to be forced to ditch as I had little or no fuel left. I told the crew to take up ditching stations. However, shortly after this I saw one of those wonderful homing lights and made a bee line for it. I crossed the coast of England with all gauges knocking on zero. A few moments later I flew over Driffield which was non-operational at that time. I could just make out the runway as it was early dawn and, realising I could never make Pocklington, I slapped down the wheels and flaps whilst I still had power – only to find when I was at about a hundred feet that some silly so-and-so had erected pylons all down the runway – to prevent the enemy using it. Of course, they forgot to put anything on the grass between the runways! In any event I swerved to port and did a little damage to the wing and cut off the starboard tail-plane. All in all we were very lucky and no one was hurt, thank God.

(In fact John and his crew were arrested by the local Home Guard 'who were most hostile in spite of our uniforms and the roundels on our aircraft.' When they informed the officer in charge they had left England at 11 pm the previous night he refused to believe them saying 'no aircraft could stay in the air that long!' Shades of Dad's Army.[3])

This was a disastrous night and the Canadians were angry – justly so in my opinion. Commonsense and practical knowledge dictated a cancellation but somewhere higher up the ladder someone was too far removed from reality to take the right decision. The Commander-in-Chief bore the brunt of the Air Ministry's displeasure and, reading the account by the Official Historian, one can only marvel. The effect was one of restricting bomber operations for the time being and a few months later Sir Arthur Harris replaced Sir Richard Peirse as Commander-in-Chief. Even so, and again following the line taken by the Official Historian, the root of the trouble lay much further in the past and the Command was only reaping that which had been sown during the years leading up to the outbreak of war. The future rise of the Command to become one of the most powerful and effective instruments of modern war was achieved by 'breasting a sea of troubles' but in 1941 we were wallowing. The effects of poor staff work such as that described above extends far and wide: confidence in the Commander-in-Chief and his staff is a prerequisite for a vigorous offensive whilst an awareness that time, effort and lives are wasted in unproductive sorties tends to lower morale among crews who put themselves at risk over enemy territory for lengthy periods.

The conclusion reached by Group Captain Smyth-Pigott, when writing to his Air Officer Commanding in mid-1941 that crews were becoming less eager to return for a second operational tour of duty, may have shocked authority, whilst the author of the letter, a senior officer in high standing, austere and reckoned a bit cranky by some, must have found it painful to commit these words to paper: but he was a great man for calling a spade a spade. He was referring to the body of instructors on his Operational Training Unit – an important and necessary establishment for the supply of replacement crews to front line squadrons – normally staffed by pilots and navigators with a full tour of operations under their belts who worked out their 'rest period' of at least six months by passing on the benefit of their experience to the men coming from training airfields overseas. I think the term 'less eager' was well chosen for it was never anything more than that and as far as I am aware there was no dodging the column. I recall a warm summer evening when a few of us gathered in the King's Arms Hotel in Bicester and this very subject came under discussion; and one of my very best friends, an instructor at a nearby OTU, assured me 'they'll never get me back for another tour – not on your life' but he went just the same and lost his life over Brest a month or so afterwards, attacking the *Scharnhorst* and *Gneisenau*.

The night bombing offensive through 1941 was a hit and miss affair and until Mr Butt[4] produced his shattering report everyone remained happy in the belief that most of the high explosive discharged over Germany was finding the mark. Well, it wasn't and the loss of valuable lives went on in ignorance of the facts. We were only too ready to seize on the statement that the bomb aimer 'believed' he had the target in his sights whereas Mr Butt proved conclusively ours was a cloud-cuckoo world and quite frequently missed it by miles. The enemy had the edge on us in terms of defence: his massed gun batteries and searchlights complemented the frustration of men struggling to find and strike a given target with equipment only one stage removed from that employed by their fathers in Lord Trenchard's Independent Air Force of the First World War. Nevertheless, Bomber Command conducted an offensive into the enemy's homeland at a time when no alternative could be found, compelling him to divert immense resources to oppose it; whilst the gain in morale to a nation fighting for its life needs no emphasis. Our crews displayed a gallantry and devotion to duty which was second to none but it took time to rid ourselves of 'ideas which we conceived before we had the chance to learn from experience' – in the words of the man who conceived the idea of a marking force and fought with might and main to see it established – Air Vice-Marshal Sydney Bufton. Bomber Command turned the corner in January 1943 – more than three years after war broke out – when, thanks to the efforts of the back room boys, a pattern of attack began to emerge – which ultimately devastated whole cities, embracing a violence and precision hitherto undreamed of. But it was a long time coming and for the cause of this delay we need to go back to the 'thirties – to attitudes stemming from a reluctance to grasp the opportunities presented by advances in civil aviation on the one hand and a study of the potential enemy on the other, whose activites in Spain after 1936 when his Condor Legion proved the ground for the expanding Luftwaffe indicated new trends in air warfare. The foregoing has been neatly analysed by the professional writers such as Anthony Verrier and by Noble Frankland in the Official History of the

Flight Sergeant John Searby marries Eva Rowland on 29th November 1939 at Eynsham, near Oxford and a few miles from the airfield at Bicester to which his squadron had been moved on the outbreak of war. He was commissioned soon after this time.

John Searby

Bombing Offensive but a 'worm's eye view' from one who was part of the struggling Bomber Command in those days may contribute something of interest.

Any young man who learned to fly and joined a squadron in the mid-thirties onwards could count himself fortunate in his choice. This was a time of high morale and marked esprit stimulated by the prospect of a worthwhile job, a good standard of living, a benevolent attitude on the part of authority and abundant scope for sport and athletics. The enthusiastic response to the offer of Short Service Commissions and the opportunities to join the Volunteer Reserve was plain evidence of the popularity of the Royal Air Force in that period: they came from all walks of life and especially from the former Dominions whose contribution to the expanding RAF was considerable; and the quality was of the best. Australians, Canadians, New Zealanders, South Africans, Rhodesians – one met them everywhere and every unit benefited from a mixture of individuals with such varied backgrounds. Indeed, after war broke out and bomber crews numbered five, six and seven officers and NCOs, there was universal belief that a mixed crew was the happiest. Thus there was no shortage of men, keen to fly, and the right material. The airfields were building – good permanent RAF stations – and all facilities were provided in the shape of maintenance workshops, fuel installations, transport and much more besides. True, the aircraft were mainly biplanes but there was the expectation and promise of more up to date types but in the meantime there was scope for training and no shortage of flying hours. The 'stick and throttle' boys had a field day – and nobody thought very much about navigators – because there were none!

There were few situations which could not be resolved on the basis of what was termed 'Air Pilotage' – the established mode of flying the relatively short distances which lay within the range of the simple Hawker Hind – and it was mainly an exercise in map-reading and common sense. We applied the forecast wind speed and direction to the course and speed calculator and adhered faithfully to the result. When the Blenheims arrived and a crew of three was established – pilot, navigator and wireless operator/air gunner – we began to consider the problem of navigation rather more seriously, but that didn't happen overnight. In the first place the navigator (or air observer to give him his official title at that time) was a newly promoted sergeant fresh from training at the schools springing up all over the country and since no accommodation was provided in the short nosed Blenheim for plotting the course he sat beside the pilot using the old Bigsworth chart board balanced on his knee. The result was a combined effort on the part of pilot and observer with an occasional wireless bearing supplied by the operator in the back. Even when the aircraft was modified and space made for the navigator by extending the nose the situation did not change very much and it was in this manner the Blenheims went to war: indeed, it lasted out their time and it was a miserable aeroplane for any crew to operate.

The Hampden wasn't much better with the navigator stuck out in front of the pilot in his perspex cage and he faced similar difficulties plus a sense of complete isolation from his colleagues. The 'mediums' – Wellington and Whitley – were in another class altogether; ample room for everyone and they put out some remarkable efforts after the balloon went up – but that lay in the future and in the warm summer days of '38 and '39 we flew many air exercises using precisely the same techniques for finding our way as had prevailed through the dead years of the twenties when the RAF was starved of everything from petrol to tyres.

Two years running on the annual trek to the practice bombing camps I flew as navigator to my squadron commander – leading the squadron at the commencement and arriving last to land. It wasn't remarkable; he didn't like flying, though in all other respects he was a competent CO – and his real forte was in the servicing and maintenance of the aircraft: we had a better record than any similar unit and fewer accidents. The old Blenheim was full of tricks – or seemed so when we first became acquainted – and there were many fatal accidents caused by engine failure at take-off: one engine would cut and at that time we knew nothing of what was later called 'safety speed' whereby one got up enough speed quickly to maintain control in the event of one motor failing.

Occasionally someone would pull the wrong lever – after landing he needed to retract the wing flaps – and the Blenheim would sink to the ground with the undercarriage neatly tucked up in the nacelles – very embarrassing; and it was not unknown for a landing to be made without first lowering the wheels! The transition from a fixed undercarriage biplane to a fast monoplane like the Blenheim had its moments whilst the need to get down to the business of instrument flying assumed a far more serious aspect than heretofore: greater range meant longer flights with the possibility of varying weather conditions when the hours spent in the simulator – the Link Trainer – paid off handsomely. Night flying was not popular with authority – at least it was cancelled at the first threat from the weather all too often to the disgust of the young officer pilots – and it was not until the last three months of peace that we achieved anything like a regular dose of flying and landing in the dark – which was a pity because one night exercise was worth three flown by day.

However, that was how it was in my particular squadron and in the event we did not go to war but became a training unit a couple of weeks before it all began. Frustration was widespread, but when the results of the first bombing attacks made upon the German fleet on 4th September were made known the grumbling ceased miraculously.[5] I remember that day very well and voices were lowered in the mess – if that was war, then it was not quite what some of us had in mind. Well, we all went to the 'sharp end', sooner or later, and nobody failed to give of his best whilst the shock we suffered on the day after the shooting started is understandable. We knew many of the crews in our sister squadron which attacked the enemy battleships and that fact brought it home the more effectively: to suffer extinction when the war was less than 48 hours old, without time to get used to the idea, was very hard.

There were some amusing incidents in those very early days. A new station commander arrived – one of the old brigade and tough with it – whose first question concerned the issue of gas clothing to all station personnel. No satisfactory answer was forthcoming and though it was midnight immediate action was taken to open up the equipment section and dole out the anti- gas capes, goggles and so forth with long lines of airmen, including many reservists on call-up, standing in the rain outside the main stores, having been dragged from their beds. That night I was on duty in the newly set up Operations Room and our new station commander burst in around four o'clock in the morning demanding to be shown the station defence plan and the location of various machine-gun posts around the airfield. A field telephone connected them all with the Ops Room and they answered one by one save the gunners up on the water tower. No amount of churning on the handle of the transmitter produced a response and I was ordered to ascend the water tower to discover the reason. It was a wild night and the water tower had been under construction for some weeks but the iron ladder lacked the last twenty feet to the top so that a rope ladder did temporary duty. In the darkness, holding on electric torch in one hand and clinging to the swaying rope I made it to the top to find the gun crew sleeping soundly in a contrived shelter; and the bell on their telephone was not functioning.

After waking them I returned and reported the failure to an irate group captain who didn't believe a word of it and insisted on making the ascent himself. He was pretty agile but the wind tore at the ropes and he came near to breaking his neck at one moment, eventually succeeding in getting to the platform where he questioned the corporal who stood rigidly to attention in the gale. Satisfied with the explanation he went down again and having given instructions for the electricians to mend the apparatus at once he started his round of the other posts – wet through but very determined. He hadn't been on the station more than a few hours but he had us on our toes and next day the workshops began the construction of an armoured truck complete with Lewis gun to tour the airfield at regular intervals. He intended to extract the utmost from this, his second war, and I suppose we all learned something from that. I served under many group captains in my time but he remains number one – duty before all else.

Years afterwards I talked with him in the Royal Air Force Club: he was very old then but still had some spark left; did he recall that dangerous ascent? He fixed me with a beady eye: 'Of course – every detail – you were a dam' slack crowd. God knows how you would have won the war without fellows like me to prod you along.'

In September '39 all squadrons had acquired a good sprinkling of officers and NCOs from the Volunteer Reserve – conspicuous by the gilt VR worn on the lapels of the service dress jacket: they were easily assimilated and quickly proved equal to the task. At the outset there were a few squawks arising from unfamiliarity with certain usages and routines – by no means unwelcome since they were often the cause of a little quiet amusement. Bill Eyton-Williams, a young Bedford solicitor, appeared on parade one very wet morning carrying an umbrella which on the face of it seemed a sensible precaution. He was adamant about keeping hold of it and informed a startled adjutant that he possessed only one uniform, as a Reservist, and intended taking good care of it. A pleasant personality, he was popular with everyone and after he was shot down during the Battle of France I visited him in hospital to learn he had been 'stitched' down one side by a row of machine gun bullets: he agreed it was 'tiresome' and assured me it would not prevent his return to flying. He was a good as his word and was lost over the Mediterranean flying a Wellington the following year. He was a splendid man and there were others equally keen so that in every way we gained from having them with us.[6] The contribution of the VR and other volunteers to the ultimate success of Bomber Command should not be forgotten: many came in months before the war began, leaving business and professional life and without them we could not have manned the front line squadrons; they filled the gap until the appearance of the crews from the Empire Air Training Scheme ensured continuity in the bombing offensive.

The Short Service officers commissioned before hostilities in the late thirties certainly carried the command through the first two years of the war but, by the time I joined Gibson's squadron at Syerston, the numbers were running low. The survivors had in many instances completed two full tours of operations – battle-hardened, a bit cynical and seldom separated from actual operations for long. This 'hard core' was always available to undertake exceptional tasks demanding experience, determination and sheer guts; Gibson was one and Hopgood was another. They fought shy of 'staff' jobs and the humdrum routine of the training units or any kind of reward in the shape of comfortable appointments away from the battle, contriving to remain in the environment they liked best of all. In no wise did they bear any resemblance to the 'Flying Officer Kite' of music hall and comic strip fame, but were serious and dedicated individuals who had shed their youth too quickly when the enemy was at the gate.

As the war progressed the requirement for leadership in the many squadrons under command was never ending whilst the loss rate was savage. Each heavy bomber was a complete unit in itself and once airborne quite independent of ground control: the success or failure of the mission was in the hands of a youthful captain who would see no other aircraft – save in the glare of the searchlights or silhouetted against the ruddy background of fires and explosions common to all night attacks – whilst flogging his laden bomber to the target. He dealt with disaster and emergencies as the situation warranted; being the last man to leave the stricken Lancaster after doing his best to get his crew on to their parachutes and not infrequently perishing in the effort. There are many instances – there were no rules and no one ever spoke of it – where the crew got clear whilst the captain held on to the end. Even here there was occasionally a lighter side to what was more often than not a tragic outcome. Group Captain B.V. Robinson DSO, DFC – a most experienced officer – left the Turin area in his Halifax bomber with one engine on fire after a near miss from heavy flak: the fire was extending to the mainplane and he ordered his crew to bale out before a wing tank exploded. At the time they were over Northern Italy and in front lay the great barrier of the Alps. Out went the crew leaving Robbie still at the controls when he commenced to make his way to the rear escape hatch to follow them.

It was then he observed the intensity of the fire to grow less and finally it extinguished itself so that he nipped back to his seat and levelled her up again to consider the situation. He was alone in the big bomber a long way from home with no crew and minus one engine. One of the problems confronting him was the necessity for switching over the fuel tanks as they progressively exhausted themselves – a duty normally filled by the flight engineer and in the case of the Halifax involving a journey down the fuselage. 'George', the automatic pilot, was unserviceable due to flak damage and Robbie's account of rapid darts from his seat up front to switch tanks and return before the Halifax dived out of control caused some amusement, but he got home safely across Switzerland and France without benefit of a navigator. Experience, know-how and the will to fight on saved many a crew, though in this instance the others were taken prisoner and Robbie never got the chance to explain to them since he lost his life shepherding a new crew over Berlin in late 1943. He was one of the hard core and an excellent Rugby player in the days before the war, and, incidentally, one of the best officers of his day.[7]

I joined Gibson's squadron at a time when the picture was changing rapidly, when new techniques were overtaking time-honoured procedures, when a definite pattern of attack was taking hold and a volunteer marker force was struggling to solve the old, old problem of seeing in the dark and lighting the way for others to follow. In fact it was the turning point in the fortunes of Bomber Command and the first red, green and yellow target indicators, observed by the enemy to settle relentlessly over his most vital centres of production, were the forerunners of a disaster never previously contemplated. All honour to the pioneers: we gained from their efforts and sacrifice in those dark winter nights. Many gaps still existed in our knowledge and failures were to be plentiful whilst the casualty rate would soar as the enemy improved his defences. Much has been written concerning these events and the policies which bred them – praised or assailed according to taste. No matter; we knew nothing of the high debates and decision making: we represented the final act.

NOTES

1. Loss of Squadron Leader C.E. Hill on a raid to Cologne on the night of 15/16th October 1942. Hill and his crew, on only their second operation with 106 Squadron, were all killed and are buried in the Rheinberg War Cemetery near the Ruhr. The other two crews – of Pilot Officers E.F. White (on 17th operation) and T.B. Crowfoot (on 21st operation) – suffered six deaths among the fourteen crew members.

The losses of these experienced crews were incurred on a raid which hardly touched Cologne. A faulty wind forecast frustrated Pathfinder attempts to mark the targets and a decoy fire site attracted most of the bombs. 18 bombers were lost, 6.2 per cent of the 289 dispatched.

2. The records of 405 (RCAF) Squadron show that 'Flight Lieutenant Searby' flew two operations as a passenger in the squadron's Wellingtons, to Hamburg on the night of 31st October 1941 and to Boulogne Docks one week later. 405 Squadron was flying from Pocklington at this time, being the first of fifteen Canadian squadrons eventually to serve in Bomber Command. The crew who took Searby on his first flight to Hamburg, captained by Sergeant Edwin John Williams, a New Zealander, were all killed when shot down near Wilhelmshaven on 28th December 1941, theirs being the only aircraft lost on that raid. They are buried in the Sage War Cemetery, near Oldenburg.

3. Johnny Fauquier, later Air Commodore DSO, DFC, was probably the most celebrated Canadian bomber pilot of the war. He later commanded 405 Squadron when the squadron was in the Pathfinder Force and, later still, was paid the high compliment of being given command of 617 (Dambuster) Squadron in the closing months of the war. He survived the war and died in 1981.

4. The Butt Report was a survey carried out by a civil servant in August 1941. The report analysed the results of 4,065 photographs taken over the target by crew in 100 night raids earlier in 1941. It was found that

bombing was considerably less accurate than crews had reported. The report caused major changes to be made in bombing policy.

5. John Searby is here referring to the system whereby certain squadrons were designated as 'Group Pool' squadrons just before the outbreak of war. His own squadron, No 108 flying Blenheims, was thus removed from front-line status at Bassingbourn and sent to Bicester to act as a reserve and training unit, the forerunner of an Operational Training Unit. 108 Squadron never again flew operationally from England but was re-formed as a Wellington squadron in the Middle East in 1941 and flew until broken up in December 1942 because of heavy aircraft and aircrew casualties; the squadron was then re-formed again as a night-fighter squadron, flying Beaufighters and Mosquitoes in the Middle East and Italy until the end of the war in Europe.

The first attacks on German ships on 4th September 1939 were carried out by fifteen Blenheims and fourteen Wellingtons. Ten of these aircraft failed to find the German ships in cloudy conditions; seven of the remaining nineteen bombers were shot down, mostly by German anti-aircraft fire. This was the first of several daylight raids carried out by the Blenheims, Wellingtons and Hampdens of Nos 2, 3 and 5 Groups against German shipping. The heavy bomber casualties sustained forced the RAF to abandon the concept of daylight bombing and turned to night operations, for which only the Whitleys of No 4 Group had been trained. This was the first of several major turning points in the bombing war. For Searby, it was the start of that steady loss of peacetime comrades which would continue throughout the war. Were it not for the chance designation of his own squadron as a Group Pool Squadron, he might have been one of those early casualties.

6. Squadron Leader Richard Eyton Williams, the 'Bill' Williams of John Searby's story, was shot down in a Blenheim of 18 Squadron in Tunisia on 4th December 1940 and is now buried in the Beja War Cemetery.

7. The 'lone return' incident of (then) Squadron Leader Basil Vernon Robinson took place on the instant of 18/19th November 1942 in a Halifax of 35 (Pathfinder) Squadron. Robinson lost his life over Berlin on the night of 23/24th August 1943, the first night of the Battle of Berlin, when as Group Captain Robinson, DSO, DFC and Bar, AFC and station commander at Graveley, he flew as second pilot with a new crew and was shot down; the eight men of the crew are all buried in the Berlin War Cemetery.

CHAPTER TWO

'Enemy coast coming up'

'Enemy coast coming up, sir' – The bomb aimer lying prone in the nose could see the dark line of separation between land and sea marking our entry into occupied Europe. His voice was quiet – nothing remarkable about crossing the Channel into France – and the navigator entered the precise time and place, providing a useful check on our ground speed. The night was dark – velvety – and the Normandy countryside devoid of any sign of life – a dead land patrolled by a vigilant enemy who had been watching our progress with his great Freya scanner; a radar so powerful that he observed the bomber force soon after take-off from our East Anglia airfields. A carefully planned route had kept us clear of the known defences – providing always that the bombers adhered to it – and we anticipated no trouble. Nevertheless, the German night fighter strength was growing and there was always the unexpected so, watch and ward, with the gunners staring into the night was the custom. In another hour the moon would rise but by then we would be well south, deep into France in the vicinity of Lyons, the great city on the Rhône. Around us, keeping company, though hidden by the darkness, were 250 heavy bombers bound for the port of Genoa – the target for the night.

An hour and twenty minutes after leaving the French coast we picked up the Rhône and in the faint light of the rising moon, away to my left, I saw the snow-covered peaks of the Alps. Lyons was blacked out, though imperfectly, whilst Monaco, a bit further on and our turning point for Genoa demonstrated a certain independence; it twinkled with lights from unshuttered windows. They knew they were safe from any attack by us so why worry about a few lights? The most famous holiday coast in the world lay below the Lancaster; the Riviera, with its glittering palaces where the little ball rolled around the spinning dish. German officers had replaced the wealthy gamblers of yesteryear, no doubt; and the odd bomb might not be wasted. No chance – our load was a donation to the wretched Genoese in return for providing the

Germans with excellent port facilities which nourished the sun-tanned Afrika Korps. This was grand strategy brought up to date – and very legitimate. When we had knocked out the port with its wharves and warehouses a new line-of-communication would run from La Spezia and with any luck we could take that out too. To date we possessed no more than a hundred odd Lancasters but the aircraft was already making a name for itself and the future looked rosy.

The famous daylight attack on Le Creusot had taken place on 17th October 1942 within 48 hours of my joining Gibson's squadron. Ninety-odd Lancasters flew out over the Atlantic and entered France from the west without encountering opposition and proceeded to the target – a vast armament works – at low level. This was another operation designed to exploit the Lancaster potential, and it seemed the Air Staff still hankered after using the aircraft in a daylight role despite the lessons learned from the Augsburg operation earlier in the year when the formation of twelve Lancs, led by the gallant Nettleton had suffered heavy losses. Of the twelve which set out seven were shot down, whilst the five which succeeded in penetrating the defences made a truly heroic attack at roof top height. Admittedly, conditions for the Le Creusot operation bore no resemblance to those at Augsburg where the Lancasters flew across a territory crowded with both ground and air defences.

I recall Gibson's enthusiasm that morning; this was very much to his taste and he was in the best of good humours. He liked anything out of the common run – spiced with danger and calling for that little extra in the way of know-how and initiative and, looking ahead, the Dams operation was to be a supreme example. Though I barely knew him at this time I sensed a certain restlessness in Guy on occasions; the run-of-the-mill stuff – the Ruhr and similar well pounded targets were all very well and he flew with his crews just the same but the barest hint of something unusual brought a gleam to his eye. Le Creusot was a profound disappointment and he said as much on his return – as indeed it was to our Commander-in-Chief who makes no reference to this first major 'daylight' in his own account of the bomber offensive. The flexibility and speed of the new bomber did not lend itself to the type of operation flown by the Mosquito and until after D-Day, when we could call on a certain amount of fighter protection, it was destined to follow its predecessors in the night bombing role.

At Le Creusot only one aircraft was lost – shot down by light flak at the target – but it proved nothing. There was gloom that night at Syerston for the missing Lancaster was flown by Squadron Leader Duncan Corr, commander of 'A' Flight, No 61 Squadron which shared our field – a very popular officer.[1] The fact that we got away with it at Le Creusot, and at Milan a week later, stemmed from the lack of opposition. In all other daylight encounters with the enemy we received a bloody nose, commencing with the attacks on the German fleet in 1939. Very early in the war we got a taste of what could befall unescorted bombers in daylight when under attack by enemy fighters possessing superior armament and outranging the mutual defence supposedly offered by cross fire from rifle calibre weapons in the Wellington turrets. This was their first taste of combat and the theory of mutual defence did not hold good; the enemy fighter attacked on the beam where no gun opposed them and those attacking from astern opened up at 600 yards – a range beyond the reach of the .303 Browning machine-guns. In the attacks of 14th and 18th December 1939 50 per cent losses were incurred and both formation leaders won much honour in pressing them home in the face of devastating onslaughts ... and the air marshals were finally convinced.

That we should have paid so little attention to the war in Spain is a tragedy, for it was there the enemy tried out his new Messerschmitts and Junkers dive bombers. In the late 1930s the support given to Franco was commonly discussed in the newspapers and yet the Air Staff accepted the fact that the new British bombers coming off the production line were armed with little better than pea shooters. This lack of adequate defensive power was to plague us for the entire length of the war and, in my opinion, it cost many lives. The 20-mm cannon in the German fighters was a terrible weapon of destruction and whatever the circumstances, day or night, the advantage lay with the enemy.

On this particular night one had no such worries. The series of attacks against the North Italian cities of Milan, Turin and Genoa did not rank very high in the scheme of things; these targets were poorly defended and our losses were minimal. The battle-hardened survivors of the Ruhr, Berlin and similar bloodbaths regarded an Italian sortie as a relaxation from the slogging match over the enemy's homeland, whilst, for the 'freshmen' crews, these operations provided excellent navigational experience and an opportunity to work up and improve crew co-operation.

Nevertheless, these trips across the Alps impacted sharply on the Italians who were not geared up in terms of ground or air defence to offer any effective resistance: they contrasted strongly with the furious opposition thrown up by their German partners. Left to themselves they would have turned it in much sooner but, willy-nilly, they were allied to the Nazis and compelled to fight on. Mussolini had entered into a marriage contract with Hitler from which there was no easy divorce. Eventually, there came a time when the Luftwaffe took over the business of defending these cities and from then on it was a different story. Whereas, under Italian control the guns fell silent, and the searchlights were abandoned for the safety of the shelters, the German batteries fired to the last round.

Whilst the reactions of some of the more sensitive may have been less than enthusiastic the claims of our own soldiers came first. We plastered the Fiat works at Turin and the Genoa port facilities most effectively: we knew the steady stream of war material flowing out of the port kept the Afrika Korps in being and though very little has been said or written about this phase of the bomber offensive both the Army and the Navy drew benefit. Sir Arthur Harris regarded them as a diversion from the main aim but he was more than willing to lend his best efforts to assist the gallant Eighth Army. In his own account, written soon after the war he has this to say:

> Nevertheless the effect on Italian morale was enormous ... out of all proportion to the weight of attack and the extent of the damage. Three hundred thousand people, half the population, fled from Turin after our second attack that Autumn ... and there was as great and probably greater panic after the daylight by less than a hundred Lancasters on Milan. After this series of attacks Mussolini declared in public ... it was necessary to organise a nightly evacuation of all civilians in the industrial cities.[2]

On the way home that night I overtook a Stirling flying a little below me. This was in the region of the highest peaks and the Stirling just about made it with a full bomb load whilst the return presented no problem. Apparently unharmed he was making steady progress and, no doubt looking forward to his bacon and eggs. As I came level he commenced a slow turn, dropping the nose until he was below the mountain top. In the bright moonlight I saw him make a feeble alteration of course which brought him clear of the shining peak but the nose was dropping even further until he plunged into a deep ravine to strike with a burst of flame followed immediately by large explosion which lit up the icy walls – an enormous torrent of red light and then nothing more.

It was a remarkable occurrence because no parachutes were seen – no one attempted to get out though there was time. I wondered; oxygen starvation? Perhaps; flak damage? Possibly. The aircraft appeared to be under power at the time and he may have already baled out the crew. Whatever happened death came instantly to those aboard for she struck the ice covered slope at a high speed and disintegrated. Amid the heat and flurry of a big raid one saw our bombers destroyed from time to time but this was almost outside one's consciousness – one willed it to be so because there wasn't time for reflection and every ounce of effort and concentration went into the task of getting the bombs on the target. This was different; in a peaceful setting, his job done, he went without fuss or bother to certain death.

A few days after the Le Creusot operation another daylight attack was ordered against the Polish port of Gydnia. Guy Gibson was delighted: he had taken part in a previous attempt to destroy the new German aircraft carrier – the *Graf Zeppelin* – which proved a failure owing to bad weather. As we walked down to the station operations room he spoke of his experiences: despite the weather they navigated successfully to the area and after dropping below cloud the ship was seen dimly through the trailing cumulus and blinding rain storms. Each time he made a run at her, cloud obscured the carrier and, finally, he descended to low level determined to get his bombs off though the minimum height for release was two thousand feet. Other warships surrounded the *Graf Zeppelin* directing a furious fire from their secondary armament at the approaching Lancaster:

I let down below two thousand feet on a timed run from the coast with a lot of guns firing in our direction. The cloud was lowering and I dropped to a few hundred feet when something swept past my starboard wing tip – it was a bloody great steel mast, and we missed it by inches! I pulled up and we had another go but it was just bloody hopeless and after that we lost the ships altogether – the cloud was down on the water and it was raining cats and dogs. A hell of a waste of effort and all because we never seem to get the right information on the weather. Now this time we ought to flatten that damn port and everything in it. There are masses of U-boats and it's been a thorn in our sides since the war started.

Alas, the operation was cancelled an hour before take-off and the hours of preparation were all wasted. It happened from time to time, but the business of bombing up the Lancasters – hauling the bombs from the fusing sheds and winching them up to the bomb crutches – was only a small part of getting sixteen Lancasters on the line. Fitters, armourers, radio servicing teams, oxygen trailers and fuel bowsers – and much more besides including the briefing and flight planning – all had been enacted with the utmost thoroughness then – anticlimax. This was the form and all the bombs must be removed and returned to the bomb dump to the disgust of the armament staff. In reasonable weather conditions it wasn't so bad but I have known it happen on a bitter winter's night with men cursing as with frozen hands they offloaded the big bombs.

Guy was furious over the cancellation, which was understandable, though one or two of the old hands grinned slyly: attacking capital ships at low level was about as near to suicide as you could get; and a Lancaster made a big target. Only a few weeks earlier four Lancasters were lost over the Bay of Biscay – shot down by an armed German merchantman attempting to run the blockade.[3]

This type of employment was not for the Lancaster which was neither equipped for nor had crews conditioned to sea warfare, and the loss of four aircraft was a serious blow at a time when there were less than a hundred of these four-engined aircraft available. To land a bomb on a ship was always a difficult problem and the penalties were severe for all who tried it: the losses in No 2 Group – the light bomber element of Bomber Command – were disastrous in 1941, when orders were given to halt the movement of all coastal shipping between the Brittany peninsula and Germany. Any ship that put to sea was to be sunk. The AOC 2 Group, Air Vice-Marshal D.F. Stevenson was ordered to see that this was done – and it *was* done irrespective of the cost which proved considerable. He was undoubtedly placed in a difficult position by his superiors. 'Whenever those who carried out anti-shipping sorties were to speak of them it would always be with fearful, vivid memories.' Thus writes Michael Bowyer in his exhaustive study of the achievements of our light bombers* and, since I was a staff officer at the Group HQs toward the close of this phase I can back up this statement. Air Vice-Marshal Stevenson followed his brief to the letter; his ruthless direction of his Blenheim squadrons earned him the name 'Red Steve' – but the job was done. Only a few months earlier the Blenheim squadrons had been decimated. 'France had been bad. far worse was now at hand.'

> In my opinion the only way was low level, really low level right down to the wavetops, and to attack the ship from astern. I worked on the theory, laugh as one may, that a seaman always looks where he is going and not where he's been. If the Blenheims made broadside attacks they would be under maximum fire both before and after the attack ... We aimed our bombs at just below the water line. On this attack the flak was still very intense and by the time the third ship was being attacked the guns had woken. Pilot Officer Marshall's aircraft was soon ablaze and Sergeant Dunning was shot into the sea.

These are the words of a famous destroyer of ships both over the North Sea and off Malta. Wing Commander 'Attie' Atkinson was but one of a number of outstanding squadron commanders at this time, and the most modest of men. The spirit in the light bomber Group was fantastic and despite appalling casualties morale remained high. Small units in every service seem to bring forth the very best that men can offer and No 2 Group was indeed small compared with the big heavy bomber groups. I make no excuse for this diversion; the annals of the Royal Air Force contain no brighter examples of heroism and devotion to duty than those performed by the light bomber crews.

I found Gibson very helpful though he was certainly cautious of new men. He was very forthright, spoke his mind freely on every occasion and resented keenly the slightest inroad on his authority and powers as a commanding officer. Occasionally critical of higher authority he was utterly loyal to our station commander – Group Captain Gus Walker – who was no 'fuddy-duddy' but an experienced bomber captain in his own right. Here we were very

* *2 Group RAF*, Michael Bowyer, Faber & Faber, 1974.

fortunate, for not all bomber stations were so well placed: there were a few dead-beats whose only claim to such a post lay in their seniority in the Air Force List – and they were not destined to survive for long. The writing was on the wall and younger men were coming forward who had borne the heat and burden of the bomber offensive, sitting in the cockpit of a bomber aeroplane. Guy held very strong views on this matter.

Once the target for the night had been notified, it was usual for a short conference to be the called in Group Captain Walker's office attended by both squadron commanders. To further my education, Guy took me along with him on several occasions; indeed he did everything in his power to help me settle in and I had cause to be grateful.

The plan for the night was discussed and crew quotas decided: aircraft serviceability and similar matters were raised. As for the detailing of individual crews this was purely a matter for the squadron COs and Guy would brook no interference in the selection of his officers and NCOs. I got the impression quite early that his squadron was a personal affair and Group Captain Walker in his wisdom chose to humour him whilst still retaining a firm grip on events. Off duty Guy was all for a party and never happier than when surrounded by his officers; he encouraged them to make the most of their opportunities and later on when I crossed him over something he brushed it aside with the remark, 'They have little time left and might as well enjoy it.' His tone was friendly and the matter was forgotten.

One morning he looked into my office and invited me to accompany him to the maintenance hangar. 'You'll find this interesting – it's a bombsight I designed for low level attacks.' A corporal fitter was working at the bench and he looked up as we approached, 'It's going well, sir. Be finished this week with any luck.' Guy was pleased with the progress. 'Good – I'm going to need it in the near future.' He turned to me: 'It's time we got stuck into some of the more important targets, John, and this is my idea of doing it. I designed it myself and it's going to work.'

He fiddled with the pieces of shining metal and I ventured to say that dive bombing was out as far as the Lancaster was involved. It had been tried in the past but surely the technique demanded a special aircraft built for the job? He shook his head, 'No, the Lanc can do it and I'll prove it.' He sensed my disbelief, 'Don't think this is a shit-or-bust affair – it's nothing of the kind. It is scientifically

Officer aircrew of 106 Squadron in March 1943, the last photograph of Wing Commander Guy Gibson taken before he left to form 617 Squadron, taking some of the aircrew in this photograph with him. Gibson's dog, Nigger, is directly in front of John Searby.

Bombing up a Lancaster

(*Left*) Guy Gibson, VC

(*Below*) Wing Commander Guy Gibson with his two fli͟͟
commanders at 106 Squadron, John Searby anc
Squadron Leader Peter Wa͟
Hunt

designed and just what we need.'

He picked up the bits and explained the method. It was a well constructed device with a pendulous weight attacked to an arm for maintaining the vertical, complete with a scale for presetting the height of release: the bomb aimer sighting the aiming point through a tiny hole in a sliding cursor whilst the speed of approach was adjusted on a traverse. It was all very convincing and I made some remark about the effect of acceleration but Guy assured me it would work perfectly. 'This is what is needed if we are to get every bomb right on the pin.' I shuddered inwardly; the prospect of diving into the hellish opposition of both light and heavy flak made my forehead clammy! In dead earnest he offered to take me with him when he tried it out – and cautioning me, 'I don't want the bloody group staff to know about this. They might put a stopper on my idea.'

On this particular morning he was at his charming best and we discussed the possibilities on the way back to the office. His final comment was typical: 'This will make a few of those chairborne warriors soil their pants, John.' He chuckled – Guy's views on the higher staff were amusing; he disliked 'visiting firemen' and went out of his way to avoid them. He had an immense respect for Gus Walker which sprang from the latter's fine record as an England rugby player coupled with his operational 'know-how' and, whilst he expressed himself freely on the wisdom or otherwise of the plan for the night's work over Germany, a quiet word from Gus was enough. One needed patience to handle Guy on occasions, and Gus had the right touch. The pity of it all was that Group Captain Walker would soon be lost to us following a shocking accident which nearly cost him his life.

The squadron was a smoothly run unit under Guy's command. Freed from all administrative worries he concentrated his energies on the main aim. We still had no replacement for Charlie Hill and it made little odds since Bill Whammond, a Rhodesian officer on his second tour, did the job perfectly. Long after, I discovered that Guy had resisted the posting-in of a new man and had done his best to get Whammond promoted; he failed and this was unfortunate since the man who finally arrived to fill the post was a nice enough individual – older than most and relatively senior, but not cut out for the trials and tribulations of a bomber captain, which caused Guy a certain amount of worry. He left shortly afterwards on medical grounds. In his relations with others

Gibson was scrupulously honest and not without sympathy. He would lean over backwards to help anyone in trouble and displayed at times a maturity older than his years. We continued to run light until Peter Ward-Hunt arrived to take command of 'A' Flight – and there could have been no better choice: experienced, unflappable, with a whimsical touch of humour, he cheered us all up.

At the time I took over 'B' Flight we could muster only seven full crews and these included myself and Hopgood, who had finished his second operational tour and was awaiting posting. After Le Creusot, Hoppy did not fly again until he went to the Dams behind Gibson and was lost in the fury of the light flak defending the Möhne Dam. At Le Creusot he was one of four, including Gibson, to attack the Montchanin Power Station adjacent to the main armament works and the source of its power supply. Going in at low level his aircraft suffered damage from his own bombs but he struggled back to England and got as far as an airfield near Oxford where he put her down without injury to his crew. He called me on the phone next morning, asking to be picked up, and the conversation which went roughly like this:

'Hopgood here – grateful if you will send someone to collect us.'

'OK – what's the damage?'

A pause, then the drawling voice: 'Nothing much – but she needs a patch here and there.'

'Any one hurt?'

'No, no – nothing like that – no trouble of any kind.'

We had an old Manchester left over from the days before the squadron re-armed and I took it down to Croughton airfield near Bicester to fetch them. Hoppy's Lancaster was a mess; the blast from his five 1000-lb bombs had wiped off the bomb bay doors and torn the bottom out of the fuselage in various places whilst the wings had sustained a scarifying treatment which revealed the bare metal. One engine nacelle lacked its rear portion and the tail plane assembly had more holes than metal. Yet the undercarriage was undamaged and he had made a perfect landing on the last pint of fuel from his damaged tanks.

A few months later when Gibson was given carte-blanche by Ralph Cochrane to select any crew from any squadron for 'one more trip', which meant the Dams, Hoppy was just about the first on Guy's list. In *Enemy Coast Ahead* Guy has this to say about Hoppy's effort on Montchanin:

All aircraft returned safely and undamaged with the exception of W/C Gibson's (slightly holed) and F/L Hopgood's. This latter aircraft was damaged by the blast of its own bombs, Hopgood being a little too enthusiastic and bombing from below safety height.

At the Möhne Dam all Lancasters attacked at fifty feet and it was a sad fact that Hoppy lost his life as he pulled over the Dam ...

> We could see his spot lights quite clearly, slowly closing together as he ran across the water. We saw him approach. The flak, by now, had got an idea from which direction the attack was coming and they let him have it. When he was about one hundred yards away someone said, hoarsely, over the R/T – 'Hell, he has been hit.' M – Mother was on fire; an unlucky shot had got him in one of the inboard petrol tanks and a long jet of flame was beginning to stream out. I saw him drop his mine but his bomb aimer must have been wounded because it fell straight onto the power house on the other side of the dam. But Hoppy staggered on, trying to gain altitude so that his crew could bale out. When he had got up to about five hundred feet there was a livid flash in the sky and one wing fell off; his aircraft disintegrated and fell to the ground in cascading, flaming fragments. Then it began to burn quite gently and rather sinisterly in a field some three miles beyond the dam. Someone said, 'Poor old Hoppy'.*

Gibson described him as 'a squadron type' on their first meeting: this, in Gibson's fashion, meant more than the words convey.[4]

Gibson held strong views on the responsibility assumed by officers – in fact all members of aircrew whether commissioned or not – once they were posted for operational duty. To some these seemed archaic – whilst others took it in their stride – since Guy declared that all one's time and energies belonged to the front line unit; outside influences were unwelcome. The notion that crews jumped into their aircraft with the idea of getting the job done as quickly as possible in order to get back to their wives, if they had wives, was repugnant. We fell out over this one. I remarked that it was a personal matter; young officers and NCOs had wives in the nature of things and it was unlikely the girls would go willingly back to Mother because husbands were posted on operations. Some, and not all, would accept bare accommodation in the nearby villages just to be near and it had been ever thus.

* *Enemy Coast Ahead*, Guy Gibson, Michael Joseph.

Guy liked to have his officers around him, both on and off duty; the squadron was an entity created for one purpose only – that of attacking the enemy. Domestic pursuits and responsibilities should not interfere with the main aim and he practised what he preached since his own wife lived a long way off. It was necessary for all aircrew to live on the station available at short notice but, of course, he could not make any ruling in respect of wives taking up residence in the local area. Few of the young aircrew members were married and really there was no problem of any magnitude but there were instances, and on occasions one had to perform the sad duty of informing the girl that her husband had not returned from an operational mission. When this happened I took it on myself to break the news – or sent my deputy – believing it better it should come from someone having direct contact, and who had shared the same dangers.

A two-flight squadron numbered sixteen Lancasters on the line and two in reserve – in theory – though battle damage and missing aircraft cut us down occasionally to less than a dozen. Given 24 hours respite and, miraculously, I used to think, we could be up to full strength again. The organisation whereby replacement Lancs were flown in from the maintenance units worked well and if new aircraft were not available a little juggle on the part of the group staff usually found at least one aircraft to plug the gap. With crews it was not so simple. The loss of battle-hardened men might not be made good by crews newly posted from the training establishments. It is true, that occasionally raw crews were sent out; the prefix 'Goodwood' on the Ops Order for the night was mandatory and every aircraft was pressed into service without regard for the experience of the crew. It was bad economics to throw away a new, inexperienced crew – their training occupied two full years from selection to arrival at the squadron and it was an expensive business, including sending them overseas to Canada or South Africa where there were no weather problems and no enemy interference. Around late '42 and early '43 the flow of trained young pilots and navigators was evidence of the success of the Empire Training Scheme: fit and sunburned, chock full of enthusiasm, they took their places in the front line units. Guy, to his credit, took every opportunity to break in such crews and refused to send them into the Ruhr and similar 'hot' targets until he was satisfied they were ready.

Prominent among the 'B' Flight contingent were 'the three Cs' –

Cooper, Curtin and Cassels – who bore a charmed life until Don Curtin, a young American from Brooklyn, New York, was lost over Nuremberg in the following February. A crisp, curly-haired individual who always looked as if he had just stepped out of a bath, he won his DFC on his first operation of war. This occurred in May of the previous year when Air Marshal Harris launched the first of the three 'Thousand Bomber Raids' against Cologne: an unprecedented number which might only be achieved by bringing in the conversion units plus four Wellingtons from Training Command. One of these aircraft was captained by Flying Officer Curtin. Battered by heavy flak he succeeded in dropping his bombs on the target but as he limped back to the coast of Holland he was intercepted and badly mauled by a night fighter sustaining structural damage and the loss of his starboard engine. Nevertheless he contrived to get the Wellington back across the Channel with his crew safe.

A quiet man he exuded cheerfulness and was a byword for modesty.[5] Cooper was the text-book Englishman, sturdy and unflappable, an excellent captain and much respected: he and Jock Cassels, a most likable Scot, survived the war. And there were others cast in a similar mould including Healey, a gentlemanly character newly promoted to flight lieutenant and an absolute pillar of strength. His death affected me strongly, for I saw in him an echo of the Rupert Brooke tradition – a shy individual with a philosophic outlook and a twinkle in his eye who captained one of the best crews in the squadron. Indeed, as a crew they stood out strongly since the chief 'wag' and originator of frequent sallies to Margot's Bar in the Black Boy at Nottingham functioned as their wireless operator. Michael Lumley and Pennington, the navigator, were seldom more than a few feet from Healey, the former doing all the talking until a quiet 'Shut up, Lumley' came from Healey and peace was restored. Mike was irrepressible and as the owner of a disreputable MG car he was never short of passengers to that famous hostelry.

They were lost somewhere over the Zuyder Zee on the night of 13th January 1943 when the temperature was forty below at 18,000 feet and my own gunners suffered frostbite and almost everything that could go wrong did so – failure of the inter-com, failure of the heating circuit to the rear gunner, overspeeding and consequent shut-down of the starboard inner engine and a near miss which blew off a bombdoor. All minor irritations but the night is memorable for the ferocity of the Ruhr defences. All in all it was a horrible experience: the flak was intense, continuous and deadly; a bomber blew up alongside us on the bombing run and the searchlights were a pain – locking on as we went in – blinding us and encouraging the heavy guns to take advantage of the trap they set. We got clear only to find a fire raging in the wireless compartment and the flight deck filling with smoke and fumes; a small piece of shrapnel had penetrated the roof of the bomb bay and struck one of the 'black boxes' full of radio stuff and invariably working at a high temperature.

As we neared the coast, our wireless operator intercepted a transmission which we believed came from a 106 aircraft about to ditch. This was never verified but I have reason to think he was right and it could well have been sent by Healey or by Flight Sergeant Phair for both failed to return.[6] This operation cost us five officers and ten NCOs – all experienced and not easily replaced. Sergeant Reed was shot up by a night fighter; the mid-upper gunner was killed and the rear gunner wounded – a bad night for the squadron. Phair, a superb pilot, was highly regarded by Gibson and in line for a commission: he was near the end of his tour of duty, having attacked some of the toughest targets in the Reich and invariably brought back an aiming-point photograph taken by the night-camera at the moment his bombs struck.

David Shannon completes the list of officer captains at the time I took over the flight – a youthful Australian, fresh-faced and curly-haired who was to join Gibson when he raised 617 Squadron for the Dams operation. This was his first tour of ops and later he completed a full tour of duty with 617 following the Dams raid. Under Ralph Cochrane's command David performed some outstanding feats and happily survived the conflict. All were young, in the very flower of youth and willing to kick over the traces when Guy filled up his car for a jaunt to the Bell at Bingham or to the house of a local landowner where the hospitality was lavish and the Scotch flowed like water; where a real live butler stood at the ready with a loaded tray and the sideboard was stacked with all the delicacies one could not hope to buy in the shops. Our host, a jolly man with a hunting horn jammed in his waistcoat, derived immense pleasure from such an invasion and through a haze of tobacco smoke I watched him doing the rounds. Perhaps he sensed this was the end of an era: in conversation he recalled his own war as a subaltern on the Western Front speaking of a place called Festubert and the decimation of his brigade at the hands of the German machine-gunners. So, he was one of us and that made it perfect. Twenty-four hours later these same young officers would be over Berlin! He understood; he knew the form better than we did.

At nearby Newton a Polish squadron occupied the airfield and on one occasion we all met up at another establishment similar to that described above. They were not a very cheerful lot and it proved difficult to break the ice: we had little in common it seemed. They were equipped with Wellingtons and there was a language problem: we tried hard but they weren't interested, concentrating all their attention on the liquor and staying in a compact little group the whole time. They wore an air of sadness which was unmistakable and the more they drank the less happy they became. In the corner of the room stood a magnificent grand piano and a Polish officer sat down to play: he was no mean performer and treated us to some very good stuff. Chopin of course and a fine rendering of the Warsaw Concerto which brought tears to the eyes of our Polish friends. It was all very sad. I was relieved when the pianist broke into a snappy Mazurka. Whatever their mannerisms we had to remember the Poles were the first to fight. Ultimately we had four Polish bomber squadrons in the Command and there was no lack of guts on the part of the crews though I believe they made better fighter than bomber pilots. The long stooge over the North Sea to a distant German target called for qualities of self-discipline, patience and a willingness to sit it out whatever the odds and, whilst I don't doubt their zeal, I believe their temperament was better attuned to the quick offensive role of the fighter. They did well for us in the Battle of Britain: their courage and sacrifice is commemorated in the splendid memorial to the Polish fighter pilots which stands outside the airfield at Northolt.

The task of mining enemy coastal waters and the great estuaries of the Elbe, Weser and other rivers – in fact any one of a hundred waterways and anchorages from the Biscay ports to the Baltic – devolved in great measure on the crews of Bomber Command. Immense damage, loss of shipping and sheer frustration was visited upon the enemy without a break throughout the entire war.

After 1942 a mining sortie was a recognised stage in the training of a 'freshman' crew; to go out on a winter's night – fly several hundred miles at a relatively low altitude – to find a selected spot and drop mines in the fairway leading to the port. Very little has been written about these operations, yet on occasions they called for the utmost in determination in the face of both weather and enemy action. In 1941 Hampdens of No 5 Group ranged as far as the Kattegat and the Baltic on minelaying operations achieving a high success rate and sinking many small vessels off the coast and in the narrow channels between the Danish islands. This form of sea warfare was so effective that development work went ahead to improve the weapon and means were found whereby mines were dropped at a higher altitude and modified for carriage by all bomber aircraft. The Lancaster lifted four of these 2,000-lb mines and with the introduction of radar aids to finding the dropping area the enemy was faced with a most serious threat to surface and submarine vessels alike.

On nights when the weather over Europe precluded the mounting of large scale operations mine-laying aircraft might still be despatched, flying below cloud to the Baltic or the Biscay ports. Gydnia, the far-flung Polish port used by the enemy as a training centre for his U-boat crews, figured prominently in the Navy's selections and mines were dropped in the bay where the U-boats exercised. I recall one occasion when a sudden call from Bomber Command Headquarters resulted in the hurried loading and take-off of six Lancasters with orders to lay mines alongside the mole at Gydnia. The weather was bad – storms over the North Sea and frequent snow showers were forecast – but a mixed party of experienced and 'freshmen' crews battled through the weather, flying at between 200 and 500 feet over the North Sea – across Denmark and into the Baltic to find the port and, in particular, to identify the correct dropping area off the mole.

At briefing the necessity for accuracy in placing the mines was heavily stressed; there was no room for error. The defences – light flak guns at low altitude – were the usual and perhaps worse than the guns was the number of searchlights deployed – a perfect horror for a bomber only a few hundred feet above the water. I did the briefing and I remember the stolid faces as the Intelligence Officer recounted the odds – he was a great one for the absolute truth – and the final blow fell as the Met Officer produced his chart. No one batted an eyelid. Flying Officer Price, a veteran, married to a nice little wife, and with two young children, had plenty of experience, having dropped more mines than anyone in the squadron with considerable success, was not moved. He had ranged off the Kiel coastline with his weapons, been into the Baltic and sown high explosive in the Rade of the Brest Peninsula. I saw them all off and fought my way back to the mess through pelting sleet with the thought that I might well have sent them on an impossible errand. *Eleven and a half hours later* they all returned – mission accomplished ...

'It was lit up better than Blackpool – with all those searchlights – couldn't miss it. We went in at 500 feet, just below the cloud base, with everything turned on for our benefit.'

The disruption to the enemy's coastal traffic caused by our minelayers was significant, particular in the Baltic Sea areas and on the reinforcement routes by which the enemy sent his troops to the Russian Front. The acoustic mine which came into service in the late summer of '42 presented the Germans with a unique problem whilst the variation in the fuse settings allowing up to seventy-two hours delay before the mine became 'live' added further to their problems. There were losses on these operations but very small indeed when set against the damage to the enemy's war machine.

In early December '42 more attacks were ordered against the North Italian cities and Turin received a hammering on the 8th of the month. This particular night comes readily to mind. I took off with a full bomb load and before setting course I observed an aircraft burning on the north side of the airfield: a moment later a violent explosion occurred – a 'cookie' had gone up. On our return I got the story from Guy who was standing in the control Tower watching his aircraft take off. Group Captain Walker, our station commander, was seriously injured and not expected to live: the crew of the fire tender had caught the blast and one man was killed; others were badly hurt. This is what happened ...

'K' King, a 61 Squadron Lancaster, stood in reserve some thirty yards from the perimeter track loaded with one 4,000-lb bomb and eight containers of incendiary bombs. This was the customary procedure: a last minute failure in one or other of the aircraft could be made good by switching crews to the reserve, positioned at a convenient point with the bomb doors hanging open. The tiny 4 lb incendiary bombs packed ninety to each container were held in position by a series of cross bars – electrically released over the target. As the stream of laden aircraft passed along the perimeter track on their way to the take-off point the ground vibrated causing the retaining links to move and the little bombs fell, only a few feet to the hard concrete surface of the dispersal pan. This set off the sensitive fuses and a number ignited.

The glow of the burning magnesium was seen from the control tower on the opposite side of the airfield where Group Captain Walker stood watching the departing Lancasters. He took instant action, jumping aboard the fire tender which drove immediately across the airfield. Ordering everyone else to stay a safe distance from the burning aircraft he got down from the tender and, armed with the long hook-like device carried on the vehicle, went directly to the spot – again giving strict orders that no one should follow.

The fire tender crew saw him advance to the aircraft and attempt to rake the burning incendiaries from below the bomb bay – working furiously to move the pile before the big bomb – situated at the rear – exploded from the heat. His motive was one of preventing a major disaster; the main bomb store containing hundreds of big bombs lay only a few hundred yards away and sympathetic detonation might set them off. The effect on the station and the surrounding villages might be catastrophic; the Lancaster could be replaced but lives might be lost elsewhere if the dump blew up. Unfortunately, the white heat of the incendiaries triggered off the 'cookie' and a violent explosion took place, hurling him many yards away, causing injury to the fire crew, one of whom ultimately died.

Guy told me that Group Captain Walker was literally thrown into the air but picked himself up with his right arm missing – then stumbled to the fire engine to see if anyone was hurt before he finally collapsed. This action was entirely in character. That night he was taken to the RAF hospital at Rauceby and for several days it was thought unlikely he would live – but he pulled through to continue serving for many years. There is a pleasant footnote to add. When Guy went to Buckingham Palace to receive his DSO the King addressed him: 'And how is Group Captain Walker getting on?'

Fog at base for the return caused us to divert quite often to clear airfields up and down the country. The old hands invariably picked a Fighter Command airfield if opportunity offered and when we landed at Middle Wallop on two consecutive occasions I discovered the reason. It was Guy who tipped me off – he knew the form having done a full tour of duty as a night-fighter pilot – and I was not surprised to find his Lancaster among the odd half dozen seeking shelter for the night, or what remained of it, in the comparative comfort of a fighter mess.

Fighter Command was a world totally removed from the austerity of a bomber base where the fortunate fighter boys enjoyed gracious living ... or as near as one could hope for in wartime. For a start, the airfield was better equipped for night landings, having high frequency ground to air communication whereas Bomber Command still muddled along with the archaic TR9 (an uncertain transmitter/receiver with only a few miles range) and the runway lighting made a night landing a very simple and safe procedure. An additional refinement was the group of Sandra lights forming an intense blob of light which penetrated the layer of stratus; from then on we let down into a blaze of red and green runway lighting – an astonishing sight when viewed for the first time.

And did they make us welcome? The station commander, Group Captain Stephen Hardy, even turned people out of their beds to accommodate us. I awoke next morning to the rattle of a teacup borne by an attractive WAAF wearing a flowered chintz overall. I rubbed my eyes but it was no dream. She apologised for waking me. 'Will you have your breakfast in the dining room, sir, or shall I bring it here?'

It could well have been a dream and in another moment my batman, the nonchalant O'Brien would bang down the thick cup on the table with a 'Sure, t'is a foine morning, sor – and a great pity that nice young Flight Lieutenant Brown is missing, and him such a pleasant young man.' He was often the bearer of bad news and believed it his duty to acquaint me with the facts – that man has but a short time to live ...

Sipping the freshly made tea I reflected on the fate which had plunged me into the vortex – the harsh world of the bomber pilot whose war might only end when the guns fell silent: until then most of us would follow the same dreary path across the North Sea to the enemy's stronghold. Seven, eight, nine and even ten-hour sorties, hunted and shot at by a drove of dedicated killers. Not that I had any special hate for the Luftwaffe night-fighter pilots – there was always a sporting chance – they were only doing the same job as our Spitfire and Hurricane pilots in an earlier day.

The air battle over Germany was a vastly different affair – scaled up many times and fought in the darkness. How would I shape up as a fighter boy – not very well – and it was far too late to contemplate changing my role. Guy had had a taste of it – his own choice – yet he returned gladly to what he calls the 'Heavy Brigade' and sets out the reasons in *Enemy Coast Ahead*. I can add nothing to what he has written.

The pretty little WAAF returned; she had run a bath for me and hung around so long I thought she was expecting to scrub my back. My black leather flying boots had been polished, my service-dress tunic brushed and pressed whilst the brass buttons positively gleamed ... and she was smiling happily. It seemed our battle-stained Lancasters had created a stir – nothing like this had happened before at Middle Wallop and we were treated as honoured guests. The twin-engined night fighter squadrons on the station had had little 'trade' for many months; the enemy was chary of sending his bombers across our coasts and apart from a few mine-laying Heinkels in the Thames Estuary life was quiet. Nevertheless both squadrons were always at readiness and one saw the young officers wearing flying boots in the mess with their maps stuck in the top. This caused Guy some concern ...

Bad weather at the bomber bases caused us to remain for a further night at Middle Wallop. It was Saturday and a little party got going in the evening, nothing elaborate but a friendly gesture towards the bomber crews. Guy wasn't too happy; he drank sparingly and most of the time seemed morose and itching for something to happen. He stumped up and down the ante-room and eventually joined a small group around the station commander, Stephen Hardy. The latter asked him if he was enjoying himself; a polite question but Guy was moody and obviously put out.

Suddenly Guy blurted out, 'It's your crews, sir' and he motioned towards a group of young fighter pilots nearby.

Nonplussed Hardy asked him what was the matter with his crews, and the answer staggered me.

'They're too bloody safe, sir – too bloody safe.'

A brief silence; and I wondered what was coming next. It was embarrassing and a lesser man than Hardy might well have taken offence but he remained calm and spoke quietly:

'I know what you mean, Guy – but it's not their fault there's been no German aircraft within a hundred miles for weeks. It's bad for them and I worry about it too. Believe me, they envy you. Now let's have a drink.'

It was the right treatment and Guy mumbled an apology. There was to be no 'Fighter-versus-Bomber' argument and Guy stumped off to bed, but he was around very early in the morning with a, 'Come on, John – let's get going. The weather is OK at Syerston and I want to get back.'

After thanking the station commander we all took off within half an hour and Guy went on leave for the next three days. He was under stress and that lay at the bottom of the business; he had fought a war continuously for three years – had seen many of his friends lost and the prospect of a fighter airfield with no action whatever made him resentful. In his absence I took temporary command of the squadron but one never knew for certain that he would not return, cancelling his leave and suddenly appearing in the office doorway. Towards the end of his time in command of 106 he was often away at Group or Command but we contrived to manage and he seemed satisfied with my handling of the squadron.

However, there were occasions when I lost my cool and we had a disagreement over Vegesack – the submarine base situated a few miles below Bremen on the Weser river and an important target in the eyes of the Royal Navy. Guy was on leave and I made up the battle order for the night with my own name at the top. All went well during the hours of preparation and I briefed the crews in the usual way. During the late afternoon Gibson returned unexpectedly and came into my office asking to see the crew list for the operation. He studied it, then took a pencil and crossed out my name saying,

'Vegesack! That's not for you – you don't want a lump of crap like that in your log book, do you?'

I grabbed the crew list, 'You are supposed to be on leave.'

He grinned. 'I'm now back in command; I cancelled my leave.' At that moment the Squadron Intelligence Officer came into my office.

'Change of target, sir – it's Bremen instead of Vegesack.'

I rewrote my name on the paper and Guy watched me. The Intelligence Officer vanished. I kept calm though inwardly I was boiling. Then, to my astonishment I heard Gibson say, 'OK, John, that's all right – have a good trip.' And he went into his own office. He never referred to the matter again and it was all forgotten next

day. In fact I did not have a good trip – quite the reverse – for a
near-miss shook the Lancaster badly and the aircrew dinghy came
out of the stowage in the starboard mainplane and wrapped itself
round the elevators with the result that the aeroplane went into a
steep dive from 18,000 feet down to 3,000 and I needed the
assistance of the flight engineer to pull out. Then we flew amid a
nightmare of balloons, searchlights and showers of light flak as far
as the mouth of the river where a convoy put up a curtain of the
stuff. The steel bottle of compressed carbon dioxide which
inflated the dinghy had struck the tailplane making a large hole
and we made it back across the North Sea with one engine
feathered and no dinghy should we need to ditch. That didn't
happen, which was just as well, but we heard on the Group
broadcast that Syerston was in fog and we were diverted to
Topcliffe in Yorkshire. There, the airfield was jammed with
Lancasters; it was one of few airfields clear of fog and beds for the
night were at a premium but a kindly padre offered to share his
room and a makeshift bed was brought in. He warned me about
his snoring but I slept like a log and heard nothing untoward.

Variations on the same theme – the Air Staff at Group HQ were
full of zeal, being imaginative and hard working – and a fresh
effort was made to explore the low level potential of the Lancaster
but this time it was to be by night. The target? Stuttgart, no less.
The main objective was surprise – an approach as far as the Rhine
or just beyond where the high ground begins on the fringe of the
Black Forest and quick pull up to attack the city before the
defences had time to get organised. I believe this technique to
have been the brain child of 5 Group's Senior Air Staff Officer,
Group Captain Harry Satterly, a very sound officer with a forceful
manner whilst the AOC, Alec Coryton, was willing to exploit the
flexibility of the Lancaster 'to the limit', as he put it on my first
interview.

At a few minutes after six that evening I took off and made for
the rendezvous point at Dungeness. The night was clear and there
was the possibility of fog for the return; the full moon was rising;
the white cliffs only a few hundred feet below us. This was an
all-Lancaster affair and we numbered about a hundred drawn
from every airfield in No 5 Group. This was a new experience for
most of us and, although it was never repeated, the memory of
that rooftop scramble over villages and farms with the inhabitants
standing at the open doors – easily seen in the bright moonlight –

still remains. Over the Channel I saw a few bursts of tracer and cursed the idiots who were testing their guns – a dangerous practice with so many aircraft grouped together – but I was wrong for a 'cookie' went up ahead of us and the firing was for real. The sudden bright glow followed by the explosion was typical and already the enemy fighters were among us despite the fact we were flying at not much more than a couple of thousand feet. Burning wreckage fell into the sea and we were one down before reaching mid-Channel. We swept into France at the mouth of the Somme, the estuary lying clear and sharp beneath us in the moonlight. At this point we were right down on the water where I saw a fishing boat with a man wildly waving an electric torch at the Lancasters thundering overheard: he must have had the shock of his life!

At Chatillon-sur-Seine, south-east of Paris, we made a sharp turn to the left heading for Stuttgart over country which began to undulate and rise towards the Rhine. It was fantastic – the moon was so bright and the visibility so clear that even small details showed up quite plainly and my crew were enjoying the spectacle. At the Rhine there was only twenty minutes to go and I put the Lanc into a climb to a safe bombing height – with the Pathfinder flares going down over the city as we reached the outskirts. The main target was the railway station which stuck out like a sore thumb: as we steadied up for the bombing run, light and heavy flak shells burst all around us – bright red flashes terminating in big balls of black smoke with the streaming blobs of red and green incendiaries weaving through the murk. I felt the rumbles beneath my feet as the 4,000-lb weapon and the smaller bombs left the rack, and wasted not a second getting clear so there was no photo for the record on this occasion. Ten Lancasters were shot down including the one over the Channel – no light matter and the element of surprise was missing. The flak got most of them and I saw no night fighters in the area. Searchlights were plentiful and, in general, the place was well defended.

Back over France we were low enough to read the time from a village church clock. This low-level stuff had its attraction but nearing the French coast I got up to 6,000 feet: the area was well furnished with light flak and the knocking down of an unwary or damaged bomber posed no great problem to the enemy. I discovered a reference to this particular operation in John Busby's *Gunner's Moon*. They, too, enjoyed the fun but never made it back to base – falling victim to the light flak batteries at the coast just as they were congratulating themselves on getting away with it. I attended a post morten next day at Group HQ but it was a waste of time; our losses had been too heavy – 10 per cent – and we had proved nothing save, the fact that a heavy bomber was cold meat at low level – by night or day.[7]

About this time a relief was posted in to take Hopgood's place as deputy flight commander. Eric Hayward was, I think, the largest officer, next to 'Tiny' Evans-Evans, to climb into a Lancaster, being six feet three inches and heavily built. He was an old hand with a full tour of duty in Hampdens and wore the silver and mauve ribbon of the Distinguished Flying Cross. Amiable, slow of speech and utterly impervious to all shocks and sudden 'flaps', he paid little regard to anything outside his own range of thought and action. Nothing seemed to move him; he viewed all operations as pure routine and nothing to write home about. He rarely voiced an opinion: the Ruhr was 'a noisy place', Berlin 'a long flog' and Hamburg 'very trying on occasions'. To get Eric going was not easy – he had a built-in inertia which transcended all kinds of trouble, smiled amiably, then heaved himself up and the action began. He was a superb airman, knew much about the business of night bombing and feared nothing, having seen plenty of action and, most certainly, he had no desire to win fame; that was for what he called 'the keen types'. In a sense he was the text-book Regular officer, viewing war as an extension of peacetime flying and he disliked fuss.

In addition, he retained an animal – a massive Great Dane called 'Dinnie' – which bore a strong resemblance to his master and was never very far away from him: this animal demonstrated some very odd traits in his character at times. For instance, he disliked bicycles! This was unfortunate since the bicycle was the main mode of transport on the station and every member of aircrew used one to get from the domestic site to the airfield. Dinnie would lurk in the bushes by the main entrance awaiting his chance, having chosen a strategic point since the road ran uphill and the cyclists slowed down and pushed a bit harder – then out popped Dinnie to seize the front wheel in his large jaws and a hissing of escaping air would result. This satisfied him and he would release the wheel and wait for the next victim. It happened to me and I tackled Eric who grinned and did nothing about it: this kind of joke was very much to his taste. Dogs were very popular and Guy had his Nigger who wasn't much better than Dinnie.

On Sunday, 6th December, we attacked Mannheim; a great centre of the German chemical industry which had escaped serious damage to date. The weather forecast was not good 'for the immediate target area' and was expected to improve as the night wore on but, with the Rhine to assist us, 'no difficulty should be encountered in finding our objective'. This kind of optimism provides a poor basis for launching a big force and in the event it was a waste of effort. From mid-Channel on we met thick cloud at varying heights and the further east we went the worse it became: a continuous sheet of wet heavy stuff with tops at a thousand feet. We pressed on hoping for breaks which never came until the navigator confidently gave our position as over the Rhine. I let down to test the thickness of the cloud and at 5,000 feet we came out of it. It was a black night with a mixture of wet snow and rain hampering all attempts to obtain a pinpoint, the windscreen wipers beating furiously, but to no avail.

Then it happened – as if someone had pulled a great master switch. Dozens of powerful white beams sprang at us, and we were naked against the white backdrop of the clouds: the guns belched forth flame, a carpet of flickering red bursts – followed by the crash of exploding shells, bracketing us very effectively and so close it was a miracle we were not hit. We had these novelties all to ourselves for there was no other aircraft present, and the German gunners went to it with a will. Full power, bombs jettisoned – and the Lanc rose like a bird to seek the shelter of the thick clouds but the flak followed with sickening persistence as I jinked and turned the aeroplane. The smell of cordite filled the cabin and for the first time I saw the very core of the shell-bursts – a tiny, very brilliant red flicker occupying a thousandth of a second in time.

Relief from the blinding searchlights was enormous but a new factor attended our discomfiture – ice. I could hear it breaking off the propellers – flung against the fuselage and the Lancaster was sluggish in the controls. By some quirk of nature ice had built up with a rapidity never before experienced and I shoved the nose down in a long and quite desperate dive which brought us out of the cloud – and the gunfire ceased.

We were out of the defended zone with nothing worse than a damaged propeller – the constant speed unit ran wild and the revs rose alarmingly so that the engine was shut down and we made our way back to the Channel. We landed at Stradishall in Suffolk in a howling gale where the station commander, Group Captain D.A. Boyle, made us welcome.[8]

NOTES

1. All but one man of Squadron Leader Corr's crew were killed when their Lancaster crashed into a house on this raid.

The Le Creusot raid received much publicity at the time, its low loss of aircraft indicating perhaps that Bomber Command could return to a daylight role, but, as Searby indicates, results were poor with most of the bombs falling short of the target and hitting a workers' housing estate.

2. The quotation by Sir Arthur Harris is from page 141 of his book, *Bomber Offensive* (Collins, 1947). The daylight raid was on 24th October 1942, just a week after Le Creusot, and represented a further effort to employ the Lancaster in a daylight role. The raid was carried out by 88 aircraft of 5 Group; severe damage was caused in Milan and only three Lancasters were lost, one over Northern Italy and two over France. John Searby did not take part in this raid; flight commanders were not allowed to fly on operations as frequently as ordinary crews.

3. Concerning John Searby's reference to four Lancasters shot down while attacking a blockade runner in the Bay of Biscay, this incident occurred on 19th 1942 – the same day as the Dieppe Raid! The aircraft came from a bomber squadron – No 61 – which was temporarily detached to Coastal Command. The number of Lancasters lost was actually three, not four as Searby states; there were no survivors in the crews.

The pilot of one of the Lancasters was probably a distant relation of John Searby. This was Flying Officer Archibald Leonard ('Tim') Searby from Louth.

4. Flight Lieutenant John Vere Hopgood, of Seaford in Sussex, was only 21 years old when killed on the Dams Raid. He and four of his crew are buried together in the Rheinberg War Cemetery; the rear gunner and the bomb aimer survived.

5. Flight Lieutenant Donald Joseph Curtin, DFC and Bar, was one of many Americans who had joined the Royal Canadian Air Force before Pearl Harbor. He was killed on 25/26th February 1943, raiding Nuremberg, and is now buried in the Durnbach War Cemetery.

6. The loss of Flight Lieutenant E.F.G. Healey, DFC and Flight Sergeant M.A. Phair (an American whose promotion to warrant officer came through after his death) and their crews were another example of heavy

casualties suffered by 106 Squadron in an experimental raid, with three Mosquitos trying out their new *Oboe* equipment and 66 Lancasters providing the bombing force. Essen's records show that the attack was very accurate. Only two other Lancasters were lost besides the 106 Squadron casualties. There were no survivors in the 106 Squadron crews. Healey, seen by Searby as 'a gentlemanly character' and 'an absolute pillar of strength', was on his second tour (44th operation in all) with 106 Squadron, having flown his first tour on Hampdens.

7. This raid on Stuttgart, on the night of 22/23rd November 1942, was not quite as John Searby remembers it. Less than half of the force was made up of Lancasters and the ten bombers lost included three Wellingtons and two Halifaxes. The 'low-level' Lancaster operation was only part of the raid, most of which took place from higher altitude, but the Stuttgart records specifically mention some low-level bombing and serious damage was caused at the main railway station.

8. German records confirm that this raid on Mannheim was a failure, with few bombs hitting the city and no casualties there; ten bombers were lost on the raid.

The station commander at Stradishall, where Searby landed after the raid, was later Marshal of the RAF Sir Dermot Boyle, Chief of Air Staff.

CHAPTER THREE

'A knock for knock'

Group Captain Gus Walker had been a powerful factor for morale and his departure left a gap not easily filled, though there were plenty of aspirants for such a post. Gibson viewed the future with misgiving: 'I hope we don't get a dead-beat' was his attitude and he had a point there. Gus belonged to our own generation; he possessed first hand knowledge of the fears, frustrations and fatigue which were the almost daily portion of the bomber crews. He spoke our language and dealt with our problems accordingly. He could be strict, setting a high personal standard, yet he was tolerant, appreciating that most have to screw up courage on occasions and a second chance is seldom thrown away.

A bomber station in wartime is a vast affair combining pre-war professionals with volunteers and conscripts where peace-time skills mingle with established service routines to the benefits of the latter quite often. Apart from the flying wing or 'sharp end', the support or back-up essential to the launching of the bomber element is provided by men drawn from all walks of life who are in uniform for 'hostilities only' – who sometimes need to be led rather than driven. This applies to all branches of the service but with special emphasis to men who maintain intricate machines where a single mistake or omission may prejudice lives of others.

Gus Walker was a familiar figure on his bicycle making the rounds of the station – visiting dispersal pens where the Lancasters were positioned on the far side of the airfield – where men worked all night in all weathers changing engines or performing some similar task. He attended every briefing yet left it to the responsible squadron commander – only speaking when he had something to contribute. I recall one station commander who talked absolute nonsense – liking the sound of his own voice – to the vast amusement of the assembled crews. He had never put 'bum to cockpit'; which most knew, anyway. Fortunately, such men were few and as time drew on and the erstwhile flight and squadron commanders gained promotion, we possessed a whole

68

row of experienced men at the top.

A short visit to Huntingdon made a welcome break. Here, at 2 Group Headquarters where I had worked before joining Gibson I had many friends. It was a relaxed atmosphere and relationships seemed easier by far than in the heavy brigade; and this situation never changed throughout the war. The light bomber group was about to leave Bomber Command and would ultimately become part of the Second Tactical Air Force preparing for and supporting the invasion. With the demise of the Blenheim and re-arming with Bostons and Mosquitos, better days were in store. The suicide missions which had taken a heavy toll in the first two and a half years of the war were now not so frequent but the very nature of the light bomber ops still produced grievous losses. Their work was almost 100 per cent low level attacks on defended positions in daylight; and there was much more to come in the next twelve months.

After the move of the Group Headquarters to Mongewell Park, I paid another visit in company with Geoff Eveleigh – Command Signals Officer – and at supper Sir Basil Embry, then in command of the group, was fiercely critical of what we were doing with our Lancasters. I asked him what he had in mind and his reply astonished me: 'Give me six squadrons of Lancasters and I'll take them in at low level – that's the way to make the most of them.' Basil was perhaps the greatest exponent of low level attack; his name was a byword for courage – quite apart from his skill and resolution as an evader after being shot down – and of all the air marshals he was the best at leading from the front where the action was hottest. Was there a twinkle in his eye as he spoke? I don't think so; he meant every word! He had a curious trick of making a forthright statement then thrusting his face close to your own as if defying you to contradict him.

The posting of three naval sub-lieutenants to 106 Squadron in mid-December raised a few eyebrows and the likelihood of attacks against the German fleet came to mind. Something was brewing and I asked Guy for an explanation.

'We are going to need these chaps before long; they are specially trained in ship recognition and it will be their job to see that we get it right when we clobber the big ones.' He was positively delighted with the turn of events and viewed the prospect of sinking a few German warships with enthusiasm. 'We've got the SABS and the bombs are lying in the dump – anti-ship bombs, 6,000-pounders – I'll take you over to see them.'

In the bomb dump lay thirty huge weapons – squat and ugly, each fitted with a long proboscis holding the fusing mechanism. 'These are high capacity bombs and the idea is one of knocking everything flat. The bomb explodes a fraction of a second before the main casing strikes the deck – this affair takes care of that.' And he pointed to the long tube. 'It's hopeless trying to get an armour piercing bomb inside their steel plate – too thick – but these little jobs will knock all the super structure to hell and put the ship out of commission for months.'

'And what is the best bombing height? They're not very streamlined – no ballistic qualities, I would think.'

He patted one of the fat horrors. 'Six thousand feet I reckon – should be easy to lob one on the deck from that height.' So he knew all about it.

SABS stood for Stabilised Automatic Bombsight – a most sophisticated instrument of high precision – and there were very few around; only two squadrons possessed them and eventually they all went to 617 Squadron and were used in many of the special pinpoint attacks including that made by Wing Commander Willie Tait, who sank the *Tirpitz*. The SABS was a triumph of British ingenuity and acclaimed by the Americans who had their own Norden sight, but the SABS was more accurate, if that were possible. Well, we had the bombs and the means of dropping them, plus the service of experts in ship recognition, and the stage was set for one of those ghastly forays into the Heligoland Bight or the Baltic against heavily armed warships. I breathed a silent prayer for the Royal Navy to get in and sink them all quickly.

The sub-lieutenants were splendid young men who settled in easily, joining in everything save the day-to-day bombing of German targets. This was not permitted by the Admiralty and they were to be held in readiness for their particular task. Mutrie and McGrath were tall Scots with a strong sense of fun and ready to make the best of any situation. The third NO – a quiet young Englishman-wore the dark blue and crimson ribbon of the Distinguished Service Order – an unusual decoration for a junior officer and he had earned it the hard way. Lieutenant Lee was one of five survivors from the heroic attack on the *Scharnhorst* and *Gneisenau* by torpedo bombers of No 825 Fleet Air Arm Squadron.

All three were keen to see some action and eventually obtained permission to fly as bomb-aimers with 106. They were destined never to perform the role for which they had been originally selected. Apart from a sudden flap over Christmas when the squadron was ordered to stand by for operations against units of the German Fleet – cancelled after a few hours – we heard no more. It was rumoured the *Scharnhorst* was to be moved up to Norway after repair but this was never followed up. Both McGrath and Mutrie were reported missing early in the New Year – the former over Nuremburg on 25th February 1943 and the latter in a raid on Stuttgart in early April.[1]

Successive days of bad weather – and it could be fog at base or totally unfit conditions over Germany – produced problems: to keep the crews occupied during daylight hours for days at a stretch was no simple matter. Lectures on all kinds of subjects, physical training, football matches and the like did not compensate for the lack of action. Boredom and a loss of 'edge' had to be fought off using every possible mode. Films were popular – how best to bring off a successful 'ditching' was a hardy annual – and there were the usual technical films on engines and emergency systems, but escape and evasion captured the imagination more than anything else. The frequency of bomber operations and consequent losses of crews guaranteed to the enemy a steady flow of captive airmen, and it was a possibility that it would happen to any one of us. This particular aspect of war was controlled and studied by a branch of the War Office, with connections in the Air Ministry, who sent out people to talk about the subject from time to time.

Evading capture after baling out depended on a variety of factors – including a large slice of luck – and each member of a bomber crew was provided with the means of making the best possible use of whatever opportunity confronted him. Over Germany chances were nothing like as good as over France, Belgium or Holland for obvious reasons, but it was not to be ruled out and some were successful. In all successful evasions the will to stick it out was paramount; hunger, cold and the knowledge that the hunters were out in force induced fear and not all were cast in the same mould. To bale out over the Ruhr in 1943 or later might well end in summary execution at the hands of an infuriated mob – driven mad by the devastation and death attending our attacks. If the mob got you before the military or police, anything could happen. There could be good reasons for surrendering to the nearest policeman rather than endeavouring to find one's way out of a maze of cities where there was not the slightest prospect of finding shelter until the hunt died down. In open country one might fare better and, best of all, in one suffering German occupation.

Aids to escape took many forms commencing with the map printed on fine silk capable of being squeezed to almost nothing and hidden in the lining of one's clothing or a shoe. Tiny magnetic compasses were concealed in the buttons of one's jacket – they were made so small as to be hidden in a pipe stem – or some similar place. The neatly contrived survival pack, moulded on a slight curve to fit snugly to the body, contained concentrated food, chemical purifier tablets for drinking water, Horlicks tablets, fish hooks for landing a trout, needles and thread for repair or alteration of clothing since the first problem confronting the evader was one of concealing his identity – no simple matter. Stories of successful evasion were quickly relayed to squadrons and lecturers appeared from time to time to keep us abreast of what the enemy was doing about it. One of my friends stole a bicycle in Northern France and pedalled his way to the Pyrenees where local Resistance members guided him through the mountains into Spain. When I met Guy Lockhart for the first time at the George Hotel in Buckden he had just returned from Spain where, after successfully making it through France. He was picked up by Spanish frontier guards and locked up in the prison at Miranda del Ebro, and eventually the British Embassy secured his release. He was a remarkable character, quite fearless and more than ready to chance his arm again. Indeed, he did so, on numerous occasions, pressing home the attack without regard for the odds, and lost his life while commanding No 7 Pathfinder Squadron, Oakington.[2]

It was during this spell of bad weather that an Air Ministry officer appeared at Syerston – a man of some spirit who laid it on the line, even producing a few laughs when he finished with the routine stuff about stool pigeons, heated cells and starvation diets – the customary tactics for extracting information. Fashions had changed apparently and the enemy was exploiting a more subtle approach with pretty girls and a night club atmosphere: 'You've had a rough time old boy. Now, we're laying on a party tonight – girls and lots of champagne ... just give us a few facts and we'll ask no more questions. Then you can go and enjoy yourself.' All German interrogators spoke excellent English – even using homely phrases to gain the confidence of the captured airmen:

'We've picked up the rest of your crew – we know all about you. Wing Commander So and So is your commanding officer, is he not? There, you see, we know a great deal already. Now, let us have the facts about your radar equipment and that will be the end of the matter.' He doubted whether anyone fell for this rubbish but there was more to come. He paused and looked very grave. 'What I am about to say will offend some of you – but it has to be said. We must face the facts ... and they are that the enemy is obtaining information from captured aircrew.' There was a shocked silence – this was very unpleasant but he rammed home the lesson by naming the source, not the individual, but the bomber group.

After the war I was in touch with members of my own squadron who had been taken prisoner. One told of his experiences at Dulag Luft – the processing centre for all captured airmen where he was shown a copy of squadron orders: it was waved under his nose as proof that the enemy knew what he was talking about. This piece of paper would have most likely come from a crashed aircraft. Similarly, after we had evolved the Master Bomber technique, the listening Germans recorded faithfully the instructions to the main force and an ex POW informed me of the fact. A tape was played over during his interrogation, 'They had you well and truly lined up, sir – told me they would shoot you after they had won the war.'

The equipping of the bomber force with VHF opened up fresh avenues for some of the more light-hearted and the voice of the Master Bomber was not the only one heard! One individual, and we never knew his identity, vented his spleen regularly over the air although it was strictly forbidden, telling them just what he had in mind: 'I've got a nice little lot for you, Hitler, – a great fat 'cookie' and a few 1,000-pounders, you miscrable —.' One day his voice was heard no more – they got him over Berlin, or so it was said.

Munich, the far-flung Bavarian capital beloved by the Nazis, came up for attack on 21st December, and the weather which had put a stopper on all flying over the past week changed to give clear nights with a full moon overhead. The day began badly with a letter telling me of the loss of Jack Houlston – a flight commander in a Mosquito squadron of 2 Group. In the two years preceding the war we were a trio – Roy Ralston, Jack and myself. Roy was to survive, winning fame as an outstanding squadron commander in both 2 Group and later in the Pathfinder Force under Bennett: Jack was cast in the same mould – a quiet individual, a man of up right character, utterly fearless and a born leader. Never one to make a fuss, he would stand in the background hearing everything with a slow smile as the arguments developed and, when the moment was ripe, he would drop in his two-pennyworth of sound commonsense. He was in my mind for much of the day as I went about the business of preparing the aircraft.[3] Y-Yorker had two new engines and I air-tested the Lancaster in the morning taking Sergeant Forster, my flight engineer, and Pilot Officer Anderson, the wireless operator. Guy was on leave and I had made up the battle order immediately the target came through.

After days of fog and bad visibility a quick circuit or two around Lincoln and Newark helped a lot; the aircraft was one of the first to arrive when the squadron re-armed and had survived many sorties to Germany. She handled beautifully and Forster who was destined to stay with me for many months after he was commissioned pronounced her to be as sound as a bell. Then back to briefing – a routine which never changed – and time to kill before take-off; a time when nothing seemed really worthwhile and the hours dragged past ... a dead interval which may only be compared with infantry of the First World War awaiting the whistle which sent them at the double over no man's land to the enemy wire. We lost a crew the previous night – over Duisburg – captained by Sergeant Anderson. I barely knew him or any of his crew, who had not been with us very long ... and the CO of 207 was missing on his first time out. This was Wing Commander Bain, with whom I had shared an instructor at the conversion unit: a likable officer, older by far than the average but wanting to get into the act despite his age. He was something of a philosopher and a great reader. We talked about books and the future, when the war ended. He was good company and had served overseas for much of his time so that he had a fund of stories to relate; he admired Siegfried Sassoon and lent me *Memoirs of an Infantry Officer* which I had little opportunity to return and I still have it somewhere – a reminder of a promise unfulfilled. He had not much time left.[4]

We took off at a quarter to six o'clock that evening – the moon already high in the sky – with four hours to go to the target on a direct route from Abbeville, once we had crossed the Channel. Within a few minutes of crossing France an early victory was scored by the German night fighters: I saw the tracer followed by an explosion and burning wreckage falling slowly earthwards.

Then the 'cookie' blew up and there was nothing more to be seen. We pressed on with all eyes keeping a sharp lookout. We did not usually encounter much in the way of fighters in this area but now they were all around us in conditions perfect for their task – a full moon and clear visibility. This was far too early in the game but we might lose them as we progressed deeper into France. Weaving in corkscrew fashion, swinging the tail, climbing a little then diving again for the gunners to see below the aircraft – with the wireless operator stationed in the astro hatch to cover the sky above – was the best I could do.

No one spoke – a split second counted in turning to meet the attacker – giving him a difficult deflection shot – and it only needed one shell – one small 20-mil – and he could rip a hole in the fuselage or snap a wing root. I saw more level tracer ahead but no return fire and soon we left the area to pass north of Paris where all was quiet. At 17,000 feet we flew over superb country – great stretches of moorland and forests: the moon lent a softness to the landscape which made me think it might not be so bad an area in which to bale out – concealment in those woods would be easy. Why not enjoy the peace of that Arcadian-like retreat, away from the war – from bombs and briefings, flak and the constant sweating it out among the hugger-mugger of the searchlights!

A rough shake on the shoulder brought me out of this dream of contentment: 'Oxygen trouble, skipper – can you let down to below 10,000 for a bit whilst I sort it out?'

My head was fuzzy, I felt tired and drowsy – and those ridiculous ideas of abandoning the sortie ... all stemmed from lack of oxygen! I put the nose down and soon lost height whilst the flight engineer climbed over the main spar to where the oxygen bottles were stowed beneath the rest bed. Whatever was amiss was quickly rectified and with a sense of relief I felt the gentle puffs from the oxygen economiser against my lips. I called all crew members: the gunners in their exposed positions were more vulnerable than the others since severe cold greatly accentuates the effect of oxygen starvation. All responded eventually, though the voice of the man in the tail turret was very faint, and we climbed slowly back to height.

In those early days a Canadian flight sergeant occupied the mid-upper or dorsal turret and an Irish sergeant sat in the tail. Dagg, the Canadian, was nearing the end of his second tour of 'ops' and Paddy Kerr was halfway through his first: the former was a real 'old man of the mountains' being tough, not easily disciplined and independent as hell. He had small regard for rank, would salute if he felt like it and, once back on the ground, voiced his opinion freely as to how the operation had been conducted – but, he was reliable, courageous and quick as lightning in an emergency. Whilst he may have fallen short on protocol, his whole loyalty was to the crew and, whilst he was dead casual, he was never disagreeable. I was sorry to lose him at the end of his tour of duty.

Kerr was a less flamboyant personality and the perfect foil for Dagg's occasional noisy outbursts: he flew with me on many sorties and I had the greatest confidence in him. Apart from the regular check over the inter-comm, he remained silent hour after hour, peering into the darkness, moving his turret frequently to keep the hydraulics free and never causing alarm by raising his voice – always the same even expression, when we were coned or being shot at by ground batteries. When his electrically heated suit failed on one occasion (soon after take-off) he didn't 'let on' but stuck it out for six hours and had to be lifted from the turret after landing. His award of the Distinguished Flying Medal was well and truly deserved. His place in the tail turret was taken by the dashing Preece, of whom we shall hear more as this tale unfolds.

The puny defensive power of the bomber, and this applies to all types in the Second World War, was no match for the 20- and 30-millimetre cannon of the German fighters but a pair of sharp eyes at the rear end could make all the difference between life and death for the bomber crew. A shrewd gunner could assess the precise moment to pull the aircraft round to avoid an attacker and, with the ever increasing number of the German night-fighter units, his services were vital to the success of an operation.

Since the Lancaster possessed no ventral turret, such as that carried by the American B.17s, the 'blind spot' beneath the aircraft began to be exploited by enemy using upward-firing cannon. The ploy was one of a stealthy approach, well below the bomber, to a position slightly ahead when the fighter would throttle back and pull the nose up until he was immediately beneath, unseen by the gunners; and a stream of shells from his twin cannon would be the first indication of his presence. The only method of countering this form of attack lay in the use of the 'corkscrew' – a constant climbing, turning and diving progress which could be sickmaking over a protracted period but was well worthwhile. Whilst the 'corkscrew' gained currency as the bomber offensive worked up to its peak during the Battle of Berlin, there were some who still persisted in trusting to luck; believing that if your number was up then nothing could save you – no amount of weaving or twisting – but, with the automatic pilot engaged, they flew steadily onward; willing to engage the enemy when the moment came; disdaining any deflection of course or tactical manoeuvre which might affect the accuracy of their navigation. I knew such a squadron commander – a brave, dedicated officer – who flew 'George-in' to his objective on all occasions – and lost his life eventually. Co-incidence? – maybe – but he scorned the use of offensive tactics. Admittedly, a fully loaded bomber had little scope for manoeuvre and after the imposition of a 3,000-lb overload in the autumn of '43 virtually none whatsoever. Even the Lancaster, the finest bomber of the war, stable in flight, light yet very positive on controls, lumbered through the night skies an easy prey to its agile opponent. The armour plating behind the pilot's seat had been removed to help accommodate the extra bombs and he had no protection. And so back to Munich ...

The clear weather conditions which held for the greater part of the route gave way to layered cloud as we neared the Würmsee Lake to the south-west of the city. This landmark had been chosen to provide a definite pinpoint for the run-in to commence and we found it without difficulty. The sky was full of the customary novelties – flak bursts and the cloud layer had opened to give an excellent view of the area which was packed with searchlights. We had expected Munich to be well defended and so it proved; the ground below was a mass of red blushes from the anti-aircraft batteries sending up stuff accurate for height and covering the approach from the lake. Then we were coned: groping white fingers moved back and forth across us to settle firmly on the Lancaster and· hold her, blinding me to everything outside the perspex canopy – and we were about to commence the final run before releasing the bombs. It was a bad moment; the flak began cracking all round as I stuffed the nose down and held her in a screaming dive watching the altimeter needle spin rapidly as we dropped earthwards from 18,000 feet to 10,000 in what seemed only seconds ... and they lost us as I pulled out to open the bomb doors. The Lancaster shook from nose to tail and gradually the speed fell off but we were down to 9,000 with the light flak hosing upwards – red and green blobs whistling past in steady procession.

The bomb aimer called me:

'Hold her there, skipper – steady, steady – bombs gone', and we were rid of the heavy load, but far from being out of trouble. The camera light came on and there was no escape from that miserable red glow and we flew level on a straight course across the city aware that explosive and incendiary bombs were showering down from above. The luck held and as the red light in the dash went out I swung her hard over and began a climb with full power to get clear. Not a scratch, not a mark – and I wiped the sweat from my forehead. Duty done and now for home.

Great columns of smoke rose from the burning city through which I saw the red glow of fires and the flicker of bomb bursts; bright swathes of glittering incendiaries – thousands upon thousands of tiny points of white light lay across the area – a vast spread of deadly diamonds born of the white hot magnesium lying on the rooftops and in the streets added a strange beauty to what was a panorama of destruction. Only the full moon, shining serenely over the city of Munich, provided a touch of reality. Everything else was unreal and out of time. A deed of vast proportions had been perpetrated – a knock for knock – and London must have presented a similar picture to German airmen of 1940 who sowed this whirlwind. There would be other occasions – some more legitimate than others – military establishments or Krupp-like manufacturing centres, the very sinews of the German war machine which must be destroyed – but on this occasion I took no pleasure in wiping out, in part, the beautiful and ancient city of Munich.[5] I was to go again in the not too distant future, but this particular night stayed with me for a long time. Whatever one's reactions to the bombing of cities we know that the enemy was compelled to divert a million and a half men to their defence: men who otherwise would have been at the fighting fronts and it was his own choice – that the shooting war should be conducted against the civilian population – when, after failing to defeat our fighter squadrons in 1940, he drenched London in a sea of fire and slaughter; thereby planting the seeds of final defeat in 1945. Quite apart from the Luftwaffe echelons which manned the searchlights and gun batteries, the huge array of night fighters with all the trimmings of early warning radars, and the factory backing for such defences, he was compelled to divert men and women to vast fire brigade and ambulance services in every city of the Reich.

Our way home took us between Karlsruhe and Mannheim; cities some thirty miles apart whose outer defences joined hands at the Rhine with powerful searchlights forming an enormous arch of light beneath which the returning bombers must pass. Here the night-fighters of the Luftwaffe gathered for the kill. The scene was weird – an immense stage complete with spotlights and the actors waiting in the wings for the slow-moving bombers, bucking a headwind which pulled back the groundspeed, as they approached the gauntlet passage of the river ... white dots of reflected light, the crews aware of the trap and keyed up for the coming struggle. Here, for the first time I saw the free-lances; single-engined Messerschmitts 109s and Focke-Wulf 190s mingling in the bomber stream, disregarding the heavy flak which was now in action, the guns belching flame all along the Rhine. Illuminated by their own searchlights we had no more than momentary glimpses of flashing white wings with black crosses swooping down on their prey amid streams of incendiary bullets pouring from the bomber turrets. The man on my right was hit and set on fire becoming a flaming torch which spiralled gently down until the tanks went up with a sudden gush of incandescence, but there was no time for studying the plight of others. We forged on – so slowly it seemed – until the river was behind us and the searchlights were no longer effective: the flak ceased and the moon took over once more – bright moonlight which carried no threat. We got home with only one minor incident; the pee-bag was passed for use. Normally it was kept on a hook beside the flight engineer and after eight hours in the air was far from empty. Making use of it in the captain's seat was a delicate operation and it slipped from my grasp with disastrous results.

We lost two crews from 106 Squadron that night: those of Flying Officer Cooke and Sergeant Brinkhurst – both experienced captains: Cooke was more than halfway through his second tour of duty – a fine pilot and a good officer. Brinkhurst was a typical English boy – sound as a bell, ready and willing to undertake any duty.[6] Then it was Christmas and, briefly, we put the war behind us.

On Christmas Eve there was a riotous party in the mess ante-room; the revelling was both fast and furious when our new station commander came among us ... unannounced, a tall, erect, silver-haired man of immense dignity, entirely unaffected by the racket going on all around him: Group Captain Irving Bussell. I suffered a mild shock: I had known him in the past and he was the last person I had expected to see. Since both squadron commanders were absent I did what was necessary and he responded in the most friendly fashion, asking me to introduce him to the crowd of young officers.

He came out of the ordeal with flying colours: he could adapt himself to any situation – he had done it all before – and whilst he bore an unmistakable aura of seniority and the habit acquired over many years of dealing with every type of individual from Royalty downwards, no one thought him stuffy. Presented with a whisky and soda, borne on a silver tray by a neatly attired waiter who did the job with a certain flourish, he didn't bat an eyelid though his eyebrows lifted a trifle when the young man made a deep obeisance and retreated backwards only to reappear with a vase of flowers which he pressed into Bussell's hand extending a warm welcome of RAF Syerston. This was none other than Flying Officer Mike Lumley – a great joker and slightly the worse for wear. Deep down I sensed we were in for an interesting time in the weeks ahead. Bussell's impact on the station was immediate and whilst he was no spoil-sport he intended that standards should be upheld and tradition respected.

Back in 1935 Bussell had been reckoned a keen squadron commander, looking for new ways of extracting the most from his antiquated single-engined Fairey Gordons, both in terms of operations and rational maintenance schemes to keep them flying. In the relaxed atmosphere of the mid-thirties not much was attempted in the way of night exercises save by the few 'heavy' squadrons of Vickers Virginias. In the ADGB (Air Defence of Great Britain) exercises he plugged the importance of night bombing and flew his aircraft on a series of fake missions which greatly improved the modest skills of the make-shift observers in the rear cockpits. He delivered lectures to the crews and some thought him fanciful, but there was no mistaking his zeal.

Bussell belonged to a select group of officers with a 1914-18 background, maturing through the lean 'twenties' when ten or more years in the rank of flight lieutenant was nothing special: numbers were small and promotion slow. Well versed in every aspect of Royal Air Force custom, poised and socially impregnable, he represented the older type of officer to assume command of a bomber airfield.

Alas, he was out of step; but this did not affect the day-to-day

John Searby at the controls of his Lancaster 'Y-Yorker' at 83 Squadron, Wyton, in June 1943.

The Queen with Air Commodore Bennett during the visit to Wyton.

Royal Visit to Wyton in 1943. From right to left: Air Commodore D. C. T. Bennett, DSO, HM Queen Elizabeth, John Searby, DFC, Squadron Leader 'Wimpy' Wellington, DFC, Flight Sergeant 'Tash' Goodwin, DFM, Squadron Leader 'Tommy' Blair, (unknown), Flight Lieutenant Vin Hanley, DFC (Aus), Squadron Leader 'Johnny' Johnson, DFC, Sergeant Hicks.

running of the station – well, not too much – and it was no bad thing for one's station commander to be known as a 'character – a bit of an eccentric: indeed, better by far than one who runs his station by the book and trembles every time the telephone rings with a call from higher up! Guy, when he returned from his Christmas leave, spat blood; but this was no more than I expected; his concern for the succession was well founded. He duly reported to the station commander's office in the Headquarters building and returned with a face like thunder. He was, somewhat unjustly, anti-Bussell from the start and nothing occurred to change his attitude.

The short-run offensive delivered against the submarine bases on the Atlantic coast of France during January and February 1943, achieved little save the destruction of port facilities and the dwelling houses of innocent French people: it was a diversion from the main task of destroying German industry and did little or nothing to assist the Navy battling with the German U-boat threat in the Atlantic. Sir Arthur Harris made violent objection since the submarines were protected by no less than eighteen feet of solid concrete and at this time we possessed no weapon capable of penetrating the shelters: later in 1944 the Tallboy was used with deadly effect by 617 Squadron but in early '43 the bomb had not been developed. Nevertheless, the attacks were made following a strong appeal from the Admiralty.

Sir Arthur's anger is understandable: the new radar by which we could mark the target at a range of two hundred and fifty miles to an accuracy of fifty yards was ready for use and the bomber force poised for an all-out attack on the Ruhr, within range of the Oboe equipment. Delay in bringing the device into use was dangerous since the enemy might well find methods of jamming it but the order went forth and thousands of heavy bombs fell on the area though none could reach the U-boats lying snugly in the Todt-built pens. The result of this policy was one of devastating towns like Lorient and St Nazaire, which became barren wastes where once a lively community had lived and worked. 'No cat or dog is left in these towns. Nothing remains but the U-boat pens ... So reported Admiral Doenitz, following these raids, and we could not expect the French to love us for what we had done.

Our losses in these attacks have been described as 'light' when set against the total of sorties flown – 38 bombers and some 250 trained aircrew – but they were serious in the light of what was achieved and that was precisely nothing. Politically, they might have been acceptable, though Sir Arthur, in a bitter assessment writes them off as a 'hopeless misuse of air power which could not possibly achieve the object that was intended'. To this he adds, 'the only effect was to delay the opening of the Battle of the Ruhr and the main offensive against Germany by nearly two months.' Had the Admiralty forced through this policy to include other Biscay ports it is likely Bordeaux and Brest might have suffered a similar fate, and maybe the enemy would not have been unwilling for this to happen!

At the time of these events the Navy was under immense pressure. In the official history of the war at sea the author, Captain Stephen Roskill, RN, tells of how narrowly we escaped defeat. Thus, it is sad to reflect that the 3,000 sorties flown against the U-boat bases made so small an impact on the overall struggle whereas the extra two squadrons of Very Long Range aircraft requested by the Admiralty for escort duties would have eased the Navy's burden measurably. Had we produced these VLR aircraft we might not have suffered the loss of 38 bombers since the attacks on Lorient and St Nazaire might not have been necessary. Alternatively, the missing bombers might have been employed on mining operations with considerable effect. This is pure hindsight, of course.

Whilst the Biscay ports figured prominently at this time there were others of equal interest to the Navy including Wilhelmshaven where we lost a very good crew captained by Sergeant Markland. He was an outstanding NCO pilot with an impressive record. His navigator, Flying Officer Myers, was a talented pianist, frequently in demand on those evenings when we were stood down. On one occasion he told me of his plans to go back to his studies in Vienna, when the war ended. A modest, unassuming young officer with a gentle background he wanted nothing more from life than the freedom to follow his vocation and he had hopes of achieving great things in the world of music. Thus, he looked forward to the end of his present tour of duty – and he had but a few ops to go before going on rest. For him the war was but an episode – a break from his music. Like other semi-professional people he proved a first class navigator and I remember the precision and neatness of his log and chart-work – a subject in which I have an abiding interesting.

It was rare for anyone to discuss his future – or his past, for that matter; one knew very little about people and never asked questions. There was a sameness about all of us; we met in the mess, at briefings and in the squadron crew-room; spoke a common language and, anyway, there seemed little time for anything except that which we had come to do. Crews came and went, remembered for a day or at most a week and then forgotten after they had been reported missing. Myers disappeared only a few days after our conversation and another took his place at the piano; we got through a number of good pianists in those days.[7]

NOTES

1. Both naval officers were killed – Sub Lieutenant P.M. McGrath on 25/26th February 1943 (buried at Durnbach War Cemetery in Bavaria) and Lieutenant G. Mutrie on 14/15th April 1943 (buried in the village cemetery at Sauvillers-Monliva in France).

2. Wing Commander Lockhart will be mentioned again in Note 1, Chapter 9.

3. Squadron Leader Jack Edward Houlston, DFC, AFC was the pilot of a 139 Squadron Mosquito, sent out in daylight on 20th December 1942 to attack trains in north-west Germany. His was the only aircraft lost that day. He and his navigator were killed and are now buried in the Reichswald War Cemetery.

4. John Searby is mistaken over the date of the loss of his friend, Wing Command F.G.L. Bain. Wing Commander Bain arrived on 207 Squadron on 7th December 1942 and was lost on his first operation, on 8/9th December 1942, his being the only aircraft lost from 133 dispatched to Turin that night; his Lancaster was hit by anti-aircraft fire, blew up over the target and all the crew died.

5. The photographs brought back by the bomber force showed that few bombs hit Munich on this raid; it is possible that much of the raid fell on a decoy fire site.

6. Flying Officer G.C. Cooke DFC, DFM, and Sergeant J.D. Brinkhurst were both killed. Cooke was a Rhodesian on his second tour of operations; his twin brother had been killed flying an OTU Whitley on the Thousand Bomber raid to Bremen on 25/26th June 1942. The only survivor when Cooke's Lancaster was shot down by a night fighter on the way to Munich was the navigator, Flying Officer P.C.B. Moore, later Sir Philip Moore, Private Secretary to the Queen.

7. The pianist, Flying Officer Peter Myers, aged only twenty, died attacking Wilhelmshaven on the night of 19th February 1943; he and his pilot, New Zealander Edward Markland, whose promotion to pilot officer came through after his death, are buried in the Sage War Cemetery near Oldenburg.

CHAPTER FOUR

'A fire in the belly of Germany'

The year 1943 was a year of decision and a turning point in the fortunes of Bomber Command. The skill of the scientist was to provide the means whereby the age old law that we cannot see in the dark was to be circumvented, imperfectly in the beginning, but getting better all the time. The flow of four-engined heavy bombers from the factories to the squadrons increased steadily and from the training airfields of Rhodesia and Canada what had been a trickle of replacement crews became a flood as the months went past. New methods – Pathfinder marking, wave patterns, height bands and the compression of the time-bracket over the target – produced the 'saturation attack', where the aim was one of swamping the defences and reducing the casualties. These refinements did not come with a rush but progressed steadily through the Battles of the Ruhr and Hamburg to the onset of the final assault on the 'Big City' – Berlin; and the enemy did his best to stay level, augmenting his night fighter force, improving his early-warning radars and radio countermeasures, increasing his flak and searchlight batteries.

Early in January I was ordered to spend a week at Group Headquarters to further my education. The Operations Room was run by Wing Commander 'Mary' Tudor, a lively individual possessing a ready wit and a talent for smoothing out difficulties: he had a light touch and a fund of good humour so that time passed very agreeably. The target for the night, the route and the bomb loads were selected by the Headquarters staff at High Wycombe together with the numbers of aircraft required from each group: Tudor's responsibility, among others, was one of allocating squadron contributions, rendezvous points and wave timings, all of which were discussed over the morning conference chaired by the AOC. Later a 'hook-up', with all stations connected by telephone to the Ops Room, was presided over by Tudor and it was here that his tact and diplomacy came to the fore. Each station commander wanted the best for his own little lot and Tudor contrived to keep everyone happy. With a sigh of relief he would put down the receiver, saying Solomon's problem was nothing compared with his particular task. Although we did not know it the AOC, Alec Coryton, had little time left in command of 5 Group; he was to leave us in the next month or so and the Hon Ralph Cochrane would succeed. Coryton's going was a matter for regret, since he was much respected.

When I returned to Syerston I found Guy closeted with Richard Dimbleby who had brought his recording equipment along. Subsequently, he made two trips, to Berlin and Essen, and his broadcasts were heard a few weeks later. He was a modest man, considering his achievements, and popular with the crews. Cheerful, with a total disregard for the hazards of a bomber operation, he spent his time in the bowels of the Lancaster recording for posterity the work of a bomber team.

Dimbleby stayed a week with us and Guy, who customarily foamed at the mouth over visits by such people, couldn't do enough to smooth his path. There were other visitors at this time and one stands out head and shoulders above the rest – a group captain from God knows where, save that he had an appointment with the Purchasing Commission in California. One of the handsomest officers ever to wear the uniform, he was something of a dandy; his Service Dress jacket was lined with red silk and his manner was that of a Georgian gentleman, impeccable, softly spoken and outrageously honest in his views of the way the bomber war was being conducted. He had us in fits of laughter. For instance, he had paid a courtesy visit to Headquarters Bomber Command and was present when the Staff were assessing the results of a recent attack; one which they, the Staff, including the Deputy C-in-C, voted a successful operation. He disagreed with the verdict and when asked for his reasons said quite simply, 'I was present – I saw the whole thing – and not a bomb fell anywhere near the mark.' Consternation; but he had spoken what he believed to be the truth; he had indeed been an observer of this particular operation – in a 3 Group aircraft. This happened before the advent of radar marking when it was not unusual for odd attacks to fall short of perfection. Afterwards I learned his name – Addams; though I never saw him again. His daughter gained the heights as a film actress – Dawn Addams, a singularly beautiful girl, as one would expect with such a man as a father. I gathered he was not popular at HQBC after that incident, but the truth did no harm.

On 13th January Essen was laid on, followed by Berlin three nights later. The former is memorable for the loss of two crews and the shooting up by a night fighter of a third crew, in which one of the gunners was killed and the other badly wounded. The temperature at 20,000 feet was minus 40°C and we were miserably cold. This was a run-of-the-mill Ruhr operation and my first experience of the Ruhr defences, with all the trimmings of searchlight cones and hammering flak, and most certainly not the last. We were coned on the way out, along with another Lancaster, and for a few seconds we kept company; each time I took smart evasive action he followed me – not intentionally, of course, and it was a weird exercise in gamesmanship but came to an abrupt and tragic end when they caught him with a salvo; he suffered a direct hit and disintegrated in a single vast explosion from which nothing remained, and all the time we were stark naked in the glare of the beams twisting and wriggling like a fish on a hook. It was uncanny how the flak followed us; Sergeant Robin, a young New Zealander in the tail turret, kept me up to date with the nearness of the bursts until, quite suddenly the guns fell silent and the stiff white fingers moved on to another victim. Enormous relief all round … and I dropped the nose to pick up speed over the short distance back to the Dutch coast, the Zuyder Zee below us reflecting the light of the moon at first quarter.

The Berlin attack on 16th January was a failure with thick cloud over the North Sea and most of the way to the Big City where a small gap occurred, though not for long. The new Pathfinder marker bombs were dimly observed and then it all closed over. Eight and a half hours after take-off we landed back at Syerston and a follow-up attack was planned for the next night. On this second attack 22 bombers failed to make it back to base. These Berlin ops so seldom succeeded, owing to weather over Northern Germany: our Met forecasters were badly handicapped because they lacked essential information. Later in the year, with the formation of 1409 (Meteorological) Flight, the Mosquitos flew a weather recce in advance of the operation. This was a great improvement but Berlin was rarely under a clear sky for long. Nevertheless, the enemy was kept on his toes and was compelled to man his defences, plus the supporting fire and ambulance services, representing a heavy drain on his man-power.

It was around this time that the term *Wanganui* came into use, being a code-word for a particular type of attack using small

numbers of aircraft in almost any weather conditions. If the Ruhr
was covered by ten-tenths cloud it made no odds – the operation
went forward and the crews bombed on sky-markers laid by
high-flying Mosquitos of No 139 Squadron.[1] Though we did not
know it at the time this was part of the trial of the new *Oboe* radar
soon to bring about the destruction of Krupps and similar
establishments which had eluded us in the past. No more than a
dozen Lancasters would take off for the Ruhr with solid cloud
beneath, and the crews hated it. I did a couple of *Wanganuis* – saw
nothing from start to finish save the brilliant coloured flares
released by the Mosquitos – and on one occasion battled through
appalling weather – snow and ice, high winds and a hair-raising
experience at the home airfield when attempting to land. Always
the Lancasters were picked for these horrible trips over the Ruhr
and though the thick cloud protected us from the searchlights the
flak gunners were sending up the usual barrage. When the flares
were released, a couple of thousand feet below, we sought
desperately to get them in the bombsight lens before the winds
drifted them away from the area. Since we did not know the full
story it seemed a useless exercise, frustrating and inconclusive: the
crews grumbled; and this was something new. Fortunately, these
Wanganui operations had a brief life and we were soon back to
normal 'live' attacks. However, rumour had it the AOC was leaving
– Alec Coryton, our much respected air vice marshal, was to hand
over his command – and over the grapevine the story went round
that he had objected to the dispatch of small packets of Lancasters
in conditions of bad weather. That was the story; some said he had
clashed with his Commander-in-Chief, Sir Arthur Harris, and
there could only be one outcome. He was to be succeeded by
Ralph Cochrane, then in command of No 3 Bomber Group. Some
weeks later I went with Guy to Grantham where a farewell party
had been laid on for Coryton; it was not a happy evening and
Coryton was very depressed at leaving the Lancaster Group. He
had created a singularly effective force which quickly made a
name for itself: his keen brain explored every opportunity for
'flying the aircraft to the limit' and on this foundation No 5 Group
went forward to become a byword in the command for achieving
the impossible. I remember him as a great gentleman, a fine
commander with a unique touch; he could be severe but was
always fair and approachable.

An invitation to the station commander's home for drinks

produced a light note during a spell of bad weather. Gibson and I went along to his house in a nearby village one evening a little uncertain as to what we would find and Guy was not very enthusiastic. However, we received a warm welcome though it seemed we had arrived a little early. As we stood in the lounge with Group Captain Bussell pouring out the sherry, his wife called from upstairs, 'Darling, do I hear voices? Has that boy Gibson arrived?' Guy turned puce in the face, choking on his sherry, and when our host left us us for a moment he was all for leaving on the spot. 'Come on, John. I'm not staying another minute.' Had not Bussell returned at that moment I think he would have slipped out; his dignity was sorely offended. That would have been a disaster, but Mrs Bussell appeared in the same instant, superbly gowned and utterly charming in her greeting. Guy was soothed for the present and the situation was restored. She was a remarkable woman by any standard and the perfect wife for Bussell; poised, accomplished and well informed, there was no situation which she could not handle with complete serenity. We called her the 'Duchess' – a term of affection more than anything else and she appeared on the station quite often during the short time her husband was in command. At dusk, when the Lancasters were crawling round the perimeter track her little car would appear driving straight for the down-wind end of the runway where she would wave to the departing crews. This could offend no one: it was unusual, but well meant, and followed another innovation brought about by Bussell whereby the whole station was ordered to the tarmac; crowds of non-flying personnel including the cooks and butchers from the various messes in their white overalls. At a suitable distance in front of this array stood Bussell himself – an impressive figure who saluted as the Lancasters passed to the take-off point. It was fantastic and faintly unreal but it went down well with the mob, and in some way linked the back-room workers with what was going on up front. Bussell insisted that the station worked as a whole, went to war as a unit, and each individual must feel he had a part to play, however humble.

He was an extraordinary character: his autocratic bearing and occasional eccentricities put a lot of people off but his intention was always based on what was good and proper. Old-fashioned, subscribing to all the right things in good sportmanship, manners, loyalty and the reputation of the Royal Air Force he seemed unique – in a world which had moved on from the days of the North-West Frontier wars and the Empire on which the sun never set. He looked a magnificent 'Sahib' from a bygone era. As for his lady – well, a moment was to come, one at which I was present, when 'Greek met Greek'; when neither would defer to the other in precedence and, for the sake of the respect I had for both parties, the other may not be named in this context. Bussell became an air commodore – a base commander – whilst it was said he got short shrift at the hands of the cool and efficient Cochrane (who was even more aristocratic when the chips were down!) and whose grasp of modern technology marched with the times.

Hamburg, Essen, Berlin, Nuremberg ... the bomber offensive was heating up. The successful attack on Essen using *Oboe* to mark the centre of Krupps with great accuracy was a landmark and any German target lying within 250 miles range from the tracking stations on the south and east coasts of England faced annihilation in the not too distant future. Even so, the more distant targets still presented a problem and always we faced the weather. We returned from the Berlin attack on 1st March with relatively light losses – nineteen bombers from a total of 320 dispatched. At 20,000 feet over the Dutch coast we could still see the faint red glow in the sky above the German capital.

Our aircraft straying south over Hannover and Osnabrück caught the full fury of the defences. My second visit to Nuremberg sticks out in my memory as something more than a mere entry in my rough diary. Our bomb aimer, a stolid and dedicated Yorkshireman, Flight Lieutenant Lodge, refused to off-load his bombs, being dissatisfied with the run-up to the aiming point. The shocked silence in the aircraft could be felt rather than heard as I acknowledged the dismal words, 'Dummy run, skipper!' and mournfully commenced a turn out of the bomber stream to circle the city with Lancasters and Halifaxes tearing past us at varying heights: a move which was fraught with hazard from collision and the impact of stuff falling from above.

The return to the target absorbed a full ten minutes and by then we were very much alone and a mark for every gun and searchlight. Nevertheless, we made it and Lodge performed his task with admirable coolness. As Squadron Bombing Leader he was worth his weight in gold and a splendid example to the less experienced but, I fear, his popularity with the rest of the crew suffered a temporary decline. The route out of the target area was marked by strings of flares – dropped by the enemy night fighters. It was lit up like Pall Mall and we flew, willy-nilly down this grand avenue! This was not the only occasion that I witnessed this phenomenon; yet we came through unscathed with the passage of the Rhine not far distant where the customary arch of searchlights and bursts of twinkling flak engaged the last of the bomber stream. Having learned the lesson on a former occasion I went for height and pushed up the nose of the Lancaster to 24,000 feet where neither flak nor night fighter paid us the least attention though I saw others hotly pursued and the inevitable explosions. The Halifaxes and Stirlings took a beating since the former could not make much more than 18,000 feet and the poor old Stirlings 12,000 to 14,000. We landed without incident after eight hours in the air.

Guy was nearing the end of his time in command of 106 and great events awaited him in the coming months though not a whisper of the forming of the Dams Squadron had so far been heard. He made several visits to Group Headquarters and left the running of the squadron in my hands. Six days after Nuremberg I succeeded him in command of the squadron but in that short interval my crew operated on four occasions between 8th and 12th March. On the morning after Nuremberg I briefed the squadron for Munich which was followed in quick succession by Stuttgart and Essen. These few days saw 106 at a peak of morale and efficiency; we snatched a few hours sleep, collected our mail and went back to the flights for another dose, and nobody grumbled. Never again, despite my move to the Pathfinder Force and one of the best squadrons in the whole of Bomber Command, was I to experience such a closeness and affinity with both air and ground crews; the latter toiled mightily to get the maximum number of Lancasters on the line each day. Out on the dispersal areas men worked all night changing engines, repairing battle damage and hauling bombs. Engine fitters, instrument workers, electrical staffs, bowser drivers and the faintly superior armourers formed the perfect team to keep the Lancs armed and flying. Men who would never achieve any kind of recognition, let alone a medal, but on whose skill and care our lives depended sent us into the air with complete confidence – and there were many items in the daily servicing of such a complex aeroplane that could easily bring us down ... if missed or neglected. Of course, those ground crews are now all middle-aged gentlemen but sometimes one meets them at the many squadron re-unions and it is remarkable that the spirit lives on. Indeed, in my experience we, the flying fraternity, have fallen behind and the business of getting people together, researching the records and compiling squadron histories with complementing photographic albums has largely been done by ex-ground staff such as Desmond Richards, a wireless mechanic who served in 106 Squadron and became its historian after the war. However, to return to the fray ...

On 9th March at nine in the evening I set course for Munich, conscious of fatigue stemming from the previous night's work and the demands made by the day's preparation. A supply of caffeine tablets lay handy in my jacket pocket and I swallowed two as we crossed the English Channel, the bitterness remaining long after they had dissolved. The route was familiar – Cayeux at the mouth of the Somme to a point between Karlsruhe and Strasbourg and then direct to Munich. Over France all was quiet but, nearing Saarbrücken, we saw the waving spears of the searchlights and the flicker of shell bursts. I kept well south of the frontier to the Rhine, then passed south of Stuttgart where there was much activity. The sky was clear and a bright moon revealed something of the beauty of the Black Forest region: at 18,000 feet we picked up the Danube at Ulm – a good landmark – and my first sight of this historic river. The little town lay quiet – snug – and well blacked-out as we passed the limit of Marlborough's march more than two centuries earlier and only twenty miles from the scene of his greatest battle – Blenheim. Why was such a small town so important, twice suffering occupation? Here, Mack had surrendered to Napoleon whilst the French and Spanish Fleets were being destroyed by the Royal Navy at Trafalgar.

South and west of Munich, the Pathfinders had marked a small lake from which we commenced a timed run to the city. A marked change in the quality of the opposition had taken place since our December raid: the flak was heavier and a whole forest of searchlight beams lit up the scene. Already the smoke from fires was rising to great heights and amid the clutter below the 'Pink Pansy' showed up plainly – a spot of bright colour in the centre of the holocaust. This was the latest form of target indicator being nothing more than a 4,000-lb bomb casing charged with phosphorus, petrol and rubber, and very effective. The usual swathes of bright incendiary bombs criss-crossed the approach –

evidence of a 'creep-back', a phenomenon which tended to rob the attack of much of its effectiveness and one which was never wholly eradicated despite the repeated warnings delivered at briefing. These tiny bombs possessed no ballistic properties – they could not be 'aimed' as could the streamlined heavy bombs and the ultimate solution was one of imposing a second or more delay before they were released.

At the controls one saw little or nothing of what was happening immediately below the Lancaster; the task of the pilot lay in maintaining a perfectly straight and level flight path, fully aware of what was happening left and right of him, but the man in the nose stared down through his bombsight lens at the selected aiming point – he saw everything and it was far from pleasant. He needed iron nerves at times with bursts not far off the nose of the aircraft and the blinding beams of the searchlights robbing him of vision.

Ross, my own bomb aimer, possessed splendid qualities, being cool and resolute in every circumstance, though to the casual observer there was nothing of the warrior about him: very young and very gentle, wearing glasses at all times – and blessed with a good sense of the ridiculous. I was fortunate in keeping him for the rest of my time with 106 and he volunteered to accompany me when I moved on to the Pathfinder Force – as did all my crew. His buddy was the silent Frank Forster, my flight engineer, who hailed from Sydney and wore the dark blue uniform of the Royal Australian Air Force. I never took the air without Frank; he was the most faithful and most competent airman ever to volunteer – way back when the war was beginning – to leave Australia with no one urging him to do so, though he never talked about himself. He was typical of his breed; courage, a rugged independence and a readiness to take whatever came his way; he was a tower of strength.

As for the crews one eminent writer has summed up the character of their task as being 'shot with fear, fatigue, determination and – very occasionally – professional interest'. This is largely correct: there was none of the sparkle of the fighter pilot's mission and the term 'ace' was never heard in Bomber Command. Outstanding feats were applauded quietly though opportunities for single acts of heroism were few; the number of Victoria Crosses gained by bomber crews outstrips all other formations but set against five long years of continuous warfare it is not remarkable. Duty in a bomber unit – a front line squadron – demanded staying power – the ability to stick it out for seven, eight, nine or even ten hours if necessary – and for most of that time they would be over enemy territory. Resolution and complete obedience to the flight plan was expected whilst flying skill and general competence in the air were taken for granted. Within the general framework of the plan of attack every captain of a bomber acted individually with no one to hold his hand.

There was no magic formula for survival but a good recipe was constant vigilance, a sound knowledge of the aircraft and a readiness to react instantly to any situation. Eat, drink and be merry was, in my opinion a stupid philosophy and on one rare occasion I removed a man from the battle order for the night as unfit to fly. The effect was massive. Someone said afterwards. 'What the hell does it matter – they are going to get the chop sooner or later.' He missed the point: I was unwilling to risk a valuable crew and aircraft, unwilling to see the devoted efforts of a whole succession of fitters, armourers and other supporting tradesmen brought to nothing as a result of one individual's weakness. The crew was a unit, one and virtually indivisible. Every sortie flown bound them more tightly together: the fact that not all were officers made no odds – once in the air they flew as a team. At this time we had no less than six NCO captains, each with a complete NCO crew and they were among the best: mixed crews were the rule rather than the exception, it could not be otherwise; an officer-captain and navigator possibly, and the rest all NCOs. The system worked very well.

On the subject of fear, we all experienced it; things which go bang in the night can be very frightening, particularly when they are close by and lethal. Most had to grit their teeth, including this writer. Some, like their fathers in an earlier conflict, said 'Well, if it has my number on it there's nothing I can do' whilst others, perspiring freely as they flew straight and level among the flak, thought only of the men behind them in the fuselage and went ahead to do the job for which they had been briefed. Nobody talked about it, but the man who does not know fear is unique.

Stuttgart and Essen completed this little quartet; attacked on the nights of 11th and 12th March. A note in my diary records a trouble-free trip to the former city save for the presence of vapour trails – a dead give-away on a moonlit night and a bonus for the night-fighters. We had no trouble but the presence of a 'dummy' twenty miles away from the target was something new. Here the enemy had constructed a dummy town of wood and other combustible materials in an attempt to draw away the bombers from the city proper. A few searchlights were positioned around it to create realism and later on, when the technique was perfected dummy target indicators were scattered among the burning fabric – an immense effort, costly in terms of labour and time, but it failed; the Pathfinders were not fooled and it may have pulled in the odd bomb but nothing more. Stuttgart cost us eleven bombers – reckoned a small price to pay for the destruction of the main railway terminus and factory areas. The return to Essen, one week after the highly successful attack on 5th March is a different story. Pricked by the extraordinary accuracy of the attack on Krupps, the enemy had redoubled his efforts to defend what remained of that vast complex and in my own experience it proved a perfect hell of a night. We put up thirteen Lancasters.

Earlier in the day Guy told me he was leaving the squadron and I was to succeed him in command in two days' time. This was very good news though I was too busy most of the day to give it much thought: Guy went off to Group Headquarters leaving everything to me. I stuck myself on the programme along with Peter Ward-Hunt and Eric Hayward and we all got off within fifteen minutes with the usual Ruhr load – one 4,000-lb 'cookie' and twelve small bomb containers each packed with 96 of the small incendiary bombs which did so much damage to this type of target. Marking was to be the customary Pathfinder method with the addition of the new *Oboe* device which had wrought havoc in Essen on the previous visit and, since the life of this equipment was not expected to be of long duration, we had been exhorted to make the most of it. That the enemy would do his level best to jam it in the shortest possible time was a foregone conclusion.[2]

The advent of *Oboe* brought all Ruhr targets within the scope and power of Harris's growing force of heavy bombers with a precision hitherto quite impossible of achievement and he meant to make the most of it. After the first *Oboe* attack he dispatched the following signal:

The attack on Essen has now inflicted such vast damage that it will in due course take historical precedence as the greatest victory achieved on any front. You have set a fire in the belly of Germany which will burn the black heart out of Nazidom and wither its grasping limbs at the very roots. Such attacks which will continue in crescendo will progressively make it more and more impossible for the enemy to further his aggressions or to hold where he now stands. The great skill and high courage with which you press home to your objectives has already impressed the inevitability of disaster on the whole of Germany and, within the next few months the hopelessness of their situation will be borne in upon them in a manner which will destroy their capacity for resistance and break their hearts.

Harris always contrived to strike a 'meaty' signal which conveyed something of his own forcefulness and resolution. Certainly, there was nothing flabby or woolly about his Orders of the Day, using plain speech with no trimmings; no references to the Deity's backing him. He took that for granted. Though he seldom visited his crew out on the airfields – I can remember only one occasion at the time I was invited by Bennett to take command of No 83 Squadron – it was impossible to discount him. He was present it seemed at all briefings and any reference to the Commander-in-Chief brought a chuckle from the assembled crews. When I adverted to the total of sorties flown by a prominent captain on one occasion – that he was to finish his tour of duty (60 sorties on the trot in the PFF!) he countered with, 'I'm doing five more for the Butcher, sir – if you have no objection.' 'The Butcher' was his Commander-in-Chief, and the crews always referred to him as 'Butch'. Irreverently, possibly, but with a degree of affection. They admired him for his ruthlessness. I don't think Napoleon had a better grasp of his men. He fired certain squadron commanders within the hour of learning of the accidental bombing of our own troops after 'D' Day.

On 3rd May I was asked to go to Pathfinder Headquarters in Huntingdon where I had a brief interview with the AOC, Don Bennett, who made no secret of the fact that he was looking for recruits. He asked some shrewd questions but did not press me to join. I had not met him previously though I knew his reputation as one of the best airmen of his day. Certainly, I was impressed by his enthusiasm and grasp of the many problems which beset the Pathfinder Force. My old friend Hamish Mahaddie had warned me in advance and after the talk with Bennett my mind was made up.

Wing Commander Searby, Commanding Officer of 83 Squadron, with his officer aircrew. On another print of this photograph, he has marked with crosses 23 men who were missing on operations.

Searby with most of the crew with whom he flew the Peenemünde Raid on 17th August 1943. Left to right: Flight Lieutenant F. Forster, DFC, DFM; Flight Lieutenant L. Davies, DFC; Squadron Leader N. Scrivener, DSO, DFC; Searby, Flight Lieutenant G. Ross, DFC; Flying Officer I. W. Preece, CGM, DFM; the seventh member of the crew, Flight Lieutenant J. H. Coley, was not present when the photograph was taken.

Marshal of the RAF Lord Trenchard talks to John Searby at Wyton.

Young Master Martin Searby cries outside Buckingham Palace after his father has received the DSO and DFC from the King.

Castle Hill House was well known to me; only eight months had elapsed since I left No 2 Group for the Lancaster Group and in that time the light bomber group had moved. Likewise the Old Court House had been taken over and Colonel Campbell no longer presided over the Push ha'penny board – the swish of his kilts was no longer heard. My old friends Attie Atkinson, Teddy Frayne, Group Captain Bill Hesketh had all departed. I felt a little sad but such changes were a feature of the wartime years. There were new faces and among them John Hilton whom I was happy to see again. He was a seasoned operational captain with a fine record and took it upon himself to introduce me to his colleagues. Late in the year he would take over No 83 Squadron from me and, alas, lose his life on his first sortie as commanding officer. But all that lay in the future. On this occasion it struck me with some force that every member of Bennett's staff had been in the battle – no one was appointed for his good looks or special connections but solely on the basis of his achievements. They came from every group in Bomber Command and all were volunteers.

At this time I was at the end of my operational tour and in the ordinary way would have taken end-of-tour leave – a small factor in coming to a decision but it could be important. I was not aware of any vacancy for a squadron commander in Bennett's Group and I was content to continue with 106 until some time in the future when a move to the PFF might be ordered.

On the following night I set out on what was to be my last sortie with 106 though I did not know it; this was a Ruhr operation and the target was the city of Dortmund.

Dortmund, most easterly of the Ruhr cities, supplied the German Army with the vaunted Tiger tanks among other things: it was long overdue for a clobbering and a massive attack by 600 bombers was launched on 4th May. This highly successful operation is memorable for the packed searchlight defences we encountered and the swift response by the heavy ground batteries to the 'conning' of individual aircraft. This can be attributed in part to the fact that the defences were more concentrated on the periphery of the Ruhr district but, whatever the reason, the display was fantastic. Blue master beams probed the night sky and locked on, to be followed instantly by twenty dazzling white beams with the flak shells coming up thick and fast to catch the bomber.

We were coned early in the approach and took violent action, losing valuable height in the process, but escaped without damage and went into the target on a steady run with the Pathfinder marker clear in the bombsights. Many bombers were destroyed over the city through the action of the searchlight teams and we fought our way out to the Dutch Coast thankful to leave that hellish scene behind us. Over the Zuyder Zee I saw level tracer and the death of a bomber which burned brightly for a few seconds before disintegrating – the burning wreckage sinking slowly to the water and any one who got out of that lot would have to swim for it: but I doubt very much the possibility of survival from such an attack.

On that night the then commanding officer of No 83 PFF Squadron was killed and a day or two later I sat in what had been his chair: I had not met him though we shared the same novelties on that occasion. He had been in command only three months and, strangely, left nothing of himself behind.[3] When I took over 'B' Flight in 106 Squadron, the influence of the previous occupant stayed with me for quite a while – in fact I began to doubt whether I would ever get rid of him, so firmly had he stamped his personality on 'B' Flight. The blue woollen scarf left hanging in the steel clothing locker and the doodles on the ancient blotting pad remained: I never knew him but an ambience hung over the battered teak desk for many weeks. There would be no echoes in 83 Squadron – all was new.

Another aspect of this night was the German raid on Norwich. As we flew home to make a landfall between Yarmouth and Cromer the enemy was bombing the city: the superb 'chandelier' flares – brilliant clusters of intense white light – laid bare the every corner of the ancient town. This was a truly remarkable spectacle. The Royal Air Force possessed nothing as good as these inverted pyramids of great power – and we sorely needed something better than the type of flare in current use.

I drew nearer, fascinated by what was going on. The German marker squadron – KG 100 – was dropping the flares for the following crews and whilst I had every sympathy for the citizens I envied the enemy the possession of these grape-like illuminators. This was a leaf we might well steal from the enemy's book though we had done very well with our radars and, of course, the opposition boasted nothing to touch our heavy bombers. Which was just as well. The Luftwaffe was geared to the needs of the German Army and in that role had achieved success: the lessons learned in Spain had been put to good use and the break-through in May of 1940 was as much a victory for the Luftwaffe as it was for the Wehrmacht since the former cleared the way with its Stukas – dive bombers. The lumbering Heinkels and Dorniers which attacked London in daylight were cold meat for the Hurricanes and Spitfires whilst the one four-engined bomber they developed – the Heinkel 177 – was a failure from first to last.

There was little or no opposition to this German bomber attack – I did not see a single gun fired, though some might well have done so – and how different a picture it presented to the holocaust we had left behind us? KG 100 had it easy. As for our night fighters, they may well have been here but I saw no aircraft fall to the ground in flames. It appeared to be a very one sided affair calling for no great feats of 'press-on' by the attackers and we continued to our home airfield somewhat astonished. To be fair to our defences, this raid was a quick run-in from the coast and out again bearing no resemblance to the long haul across German territory or over Occupied Europe necessary to get at the objective – which was the lot of Bomber Command nine times out of ten, with all the advantages going to the opposition who could prepare and maintain their attacks over great stretches of country to the target and repeat the dose on the way out.

I did not leave Syerston without a pang or two: I had many friends both in the squadron and in the headquarters staff. Immense goodwill and a lot of help from people almost totally unconnected with the immediate battle had been my experience in the eight months I had served on the station.

Bussell's successor as station commander was a happy choice. Group Captain Odbert, a well known rugby scrum-half before the war, knew little of operations at station level, but this was more than compensated by his friendliness and ability to understand our problems. Though I knew him only for a short while I had the greatest admiration for his character: of a quiet disposition he was inflexible in all matters affecting the running of the station and backed his squadron commanders to the hilt. He was another 'Gus' Walker and we were fortunate to have him. Alas, he was killed in a flying accident at Fulbeck soon after I went to the Pathfinder Force and I attended his funeral in Newark where the church was packed with officers and men from Syerston. 'Oddie' was much liked.

Ronnie Baxter took over as squadron commander of 106; an old friend and I could not have wished for a better successor. He survived the war, though we did not meet again for several years until I dropped into a pub one day somewhere in Cornwall to discover Ronnie testing the local brew. It seemed we had parted only the previous week for he looked up with a, 'Hello, John; I owe you a drink – that was a pretty good squadron you left me. What'll you have?'

NOTES

1. John Searby has made a slight error here. The Mosquito squadron carrying out these *Oboe* marking trials was No 109, soon to be joined by 105 Squadron. As for 'Wanganui', this term was later used by the Pathfinders for their standard blind marking method whenever the ground was covered by cloud.

2. With regard to the expectation that the Germans would jam or otherwise interfere with the *Oboe* beams, in fact they never succeeded in doing so. *Oboe* remained in use until the end of the war, providing accurate signals by which Mosquito Pathfinders could mark targets, but only within range of the device, its limitation being the curvature of the earth. But the whole of the industrial Ruhr was within range of *Oboe* and the period which John Searby now describes saw a series of highly effective raids on targets there, this period becoming known as the Battle of the Ruhr.

3. The lost commander of 83 Squadron was Wing Commander J.R. Gillman, shot down over Dortmund on the night of 4/5th May 1943, flying as second pilot with what the Squadron Operations Record Book (Public Record Office AIR 27/687) describes as 'an exceptionally keen volunteer crew'. The Record Book also comments on Wing Commander Gillman as being 'exceptionally well liked on the squadron'; it was his fourth operational flight. The crew were all killed and are buried in the Reichswald War Cemetery.

CHAPTER FIVE

'The Ruhr once again'

The Pathfinder Force came into being after a struggle between the Air Staff in Whitehall who wanted it and the Bomber Barons who didn't; whilst the backwash remained long after the policy was forced through. None of this was known to me when I left No 5 Group to join Bennett and the creation of a marking echelon seemed to be a most logical advance in improving the accuracy of our attacks. I never had cause to change this belief and, though I encountered criticism of both Pathfinder Force and its commander, it was water off a duck's back. Every man is entitled to his own opinion but once the decision has been taken then all should pull together and there must be an end to carping and sniping.

The solid core of the command – the established bomber groups – had been working up for almost three years when the PFF was established at Wyton: each possessed its own commander and staff, had developed its own methods, had set its own standards and created its own personalities both at the Group headquarters and out on the stations. The 'Old Boy' net was as effective as in any other walk of life and loyalties were strong. Nearly twenty years after the war ended I received a Christmas card from an old friend – a company director – who wished me well. At the foot of the card he had scrawled '3 Group for ever' and I think this makes the point.

The group commanders – often known as the 'Bomber Barons' – were powerful men enjoying a considerable degree of autonomy within their own groups and most had occupied their seats for long periods. Changes were rare, whilst they had risen to high rank over many years of service at home and overseas. Air Vice-Marshal John Baldwin commanded No 3 Bomber Group for three years and Air Vice-Marshal Roderick Carr, who led 4 Group for an even longer period: each was a well-loved figure with first hand knowledge of every officer filling a responsible post and possessing a shrewd assessment of the capability of the many squadrons under command. Frequent personal visits complemented by detailed staff reports kept them abreast of events out on the stations and each fought like a lion for his own: the group was a kind of 'family' and the Air Officer Commanding acquired the status of a 'father figure'. No officer succeeded in obtaining an appointment on a group staff and, perhaps more importantly, to the command of a flight or squadron save with the fullest approval of the AOC. Thus, the solidity and integrity of the group was maintained against all comers and its reputation in all matters pertaining to operations jealously guarded. Each group believed it possessed the necessary skill and experience to undertake any task: the idea that anyone else could do it better was distasteful and rejected. 'Group thinking' was kept securely locked within the particular headquarters and not even staff officers from High Wycombe could be sure of obtaining information in certain matters. 'We don't tell them anything ...' was the remark of one officer to me when I asked if the matter under discussion had been referred to Headquarters Bomber Command Staff. 'We don't want those people fishing round up here!'

Against a barrier of conservatism such as this one begins to appreciate the difficulties attending the rise of the entirely new Pathfinder Group with a youthful and very junior air commodore at its head and the fact that he was an airman who had attained international status long before he took command of a 4 Group squadron made only a small impact. If he was to get any help in the first instance it would come from his former AOC, Roderick Carr, and it is on record that this group commander was indeed the one to provide it ungrudgingly. Here the 'Old Boy' net operated in Bennett's favour since he had commanded a squadron with distinction in that group: other Barons were less forthcoming.

With the despatch of one squadron from each of the old established groups they retained a share in the fortunes of the Pathfinder Force, maintaining their interest and promising to keep them up to strength with the best available crews. This was an excellent compromise and in the beginning worked very well though as time went by the links between the squadrons and their parent groups tended to weaken: this was not remarkable since the Pathfinders eventually achieved group status themselves, becoming No 8 Group, which, quite properly, acquired its own mannerisms and methods as it increased in strength.

Air Vice-Marshal Bennett, as he was to become, possessed a

personality and strength of character which rivalled that of his brother barons – demanding, and receiving, complete loyalty from his crews whilst his special knowledge and airmanship could not be challenged. At the outset the Pathfinders were on trial. No working up period had been permitted, the squadrons arrived one day and Pathfinder Force commenced operating in almost the same breath with a hastily gathered staff. Overnight Bennett had assumed a tearful responsibility in the knowledge that not all were for the idea. He was young, lacking in seniority and known to be outspoken: in the words of Sir Arthur Harris 'he could not suffer fools gladly, and by his own high standards there were many fools'. Against this had to be set his high attainments and his experience as an operational squadron commander. 'We were lucky to get a man of such attainments to lead and form the Pathfinders' was Sir Arthur Harris's summation.

During the time I commanded No 83 PFF Squadron, and in common with other squadron commanders, I had many discussions with Bennett and it was comforting to talk with a senior officer who spoke my own language. He was a ready listener and never attempted to cut one's feet from under one but waited patiently until he had heard the proposal through to the end: after that he had his turn and a careful dissection followed. By reputation he was conceited but that was not my experience and I learned more from Bennett in the course of an hour than I did from others over a much longer interval: he possessed a good sense of humour and a boyishness which put us all on a level and there was no protocol but it is true that he had no use whatever for place-seekers, pompous individuals or time-wasters. He had his faults like the rest of us but we all knew he was the right man in the right place and that every day was a battle against a host of difficulties. His right hand man was Air Commodore C.D.C. Boyce – 'Bruin' to most of us and a very popular officer. I liked Boyce though I realised he did not always hit it off with Bennett: I found him fair, helpful and always friendly. He was as much part of the PFF as was Bennett and all the other characters and he was a factor for morale – a powerful one. As Senior Air Staff Officer to Bennett his was not perhaps the easiest appointment: his own record left nothing to be desired since he had commanded a squadron in the Middle East and done well in Iraq during the revolt by Rashid Ali in 1941 when the Germans sought to gain control of an area vital to the outcome of the war in that theatre.

Boyce was always keen to fly with one or other of the marker squadrons and flew with me on the dress rehearsal for Peenemünde. A Cranwell-trained officer, he demonstrated an easy assurance and was totally unflappable whilst on occasions his wit was somewhat caustic but, as I have said, he was well liked in the PFF. Speak as you find.

The famous Dams Raid which took place on the night of 16th/17th May 1943 excited the greatest admiration and interest: a magnificent achievement which has passed into history as one of the greatest feats of arms of all time. The team which Gibson led to the Möhne Dam contained the best and most experienced Lancaster crews in the whole of Bomber Command but the cost was bitter. When we learned of the casualties there was grief enough, for all were known to us since we were an ex-5 Group squadron. Eight superb crews out of a total of nineteen were lost and the predictions of a famous scientist had been proved correct but it was too high a price to pay for the temporary flooding of the Ruhr Valley and nothing will shake this conviction. When these fantastic weapons are dreamed up by the scientists one is entitled to wonder if an equal weight of thought is given to how and by whom they are to be launched.

I wrote to Guy after the operation and he replied, wishing me success with 83, his old squadron in the first stage of the war, and we did not meet again until September of the following year when I lunched with him at Coningsby where he was a member of the base staff. Before leaving he invited me to look over an aircraft specially prepared for low level marking of certain targets and we spent an enjoyable half hour discussing the possibilities. He displayed the same kind of enthusiasm as at Syerston with his 'this is how it ought to be done and with this aeroplane we can clobber the more difficult ones etc' but he appeared much changed, being quieter and somewhat slowed down. The old restlessness was still evident – he hated being in the background – and there was only one situation for him – leading from the front. We walked over to the Little Proctor in which I had made the journey from Wyton and he waved as I taxied out to the runway. He was killed the following night returning from München Gladbach.

Change of station, change of squadron and lots of new faces – it takes a little time to get settled and I had been very comfortable at Syerston. I did not get on too well with the station commander at Wyton in the first few weeks – he was all for organising the station

in regular RAF fashion and there was a minor rebellion among the
young officers of No 83 when he stopped the practice of returning
to the mess for tea during the afternoon. In fairness to the
officers, there was little else to do and after an airing of their
grievances he agreed to rescind the order. All small stuff, I know,
but little things tend to bulk large on occasions. He was a sound
officer in all respects, but a group of pilot officers played tricks on
him and the thing reached a climax with the rough treatment
accorded his gold-braided hat during a night of insobriety in the
mess. What they did to that hat is not for the record but I was on
the carpet pretty smartly. Apologies were made and things
quietened down eventually.

We had some very pleasant WAAF officers on the station and the
rules were strict; one could be entertained in their ante-room but
no officer was permitted to enjoy their hospitality after 9 pm.
Nobody broke this rule to my certain knowledge and, anyway,
there was no law against associating with these delightful girls
outside the station and on the warm afternoons a punt on the
nearby river provided a romantic setting. 83 Squadron was well to
the fore in the hiring of punts, I soon discovered – and what better
way to spend a 'stand-down' from operations over Germany?

The Golden Lion in St Ives and the Ferry Boat Inn down by the
river were favourite haunts in off duty hours and following the
announcement of a long list of Honours and Awards a party
developed to celebrate the occasion. Like most of these gatherings
it was a very straightforward affair and the real fun began after we
returned to the mess. Tommy Blair – Squadron Leader and the
recipient of the DFC – was a powerful personality in 83 and
decided it was an opportunity to discover what the new squadron
commander was made of – and whether he was worthy of the job.
The challenge had to be met. Four pints of beer were placed at my
elbow to be consumed in quick succession at a signal from Smithy
– a veteran Pathfinder who was seldom separated from Blair
unless there was a piano in the vicinity which he would play with a
masterly touch – and I faced Blair across the table.

The signal was given. I have never witnessed such a remarkable
swallowing of ale since that day – for Tommy whipped the
tankards off the table so quickly and downed the contents before I
had managed the first two. 'Never mind, sir. You're out of
practice, that's all. Shall we do it again?' I spluttered out a negative
and managed to finish the remaining tankards, which was enough,

and although I had lost the contest it seemed I had qualified for the post of commanding officer of 83 Squadron. He was a man of iron, was Blair, and a tremendous factor for morale: he supported me through thick and thin in the months that followed and I never had a better officer. Yet he was a civilian – through and through – never aspiring to anything more than his wartime role, jealous of the honour of 83 Squadron and ready instantly to take off his coat to defend it. He flew nigh on a hundred heavy bomber sorties, together with Smithy, his pilot and captain, and was the very stuff of the Pathfinder Force.

These were the men who marked the targets in the PFF and it gave me pause for thought at times: they were the Royal Air Force at its peak of achievement, with no thought for themselves but ready and willing to fly dangerous missions in all weathers in the face of a determined and vigorous enemy. And there were many more drawn from the Main Force Groups – or rather volunteers – for at this stage we had no 'pressed men'. Occasionally, I asked myself what motivated them to opt for a tough tour of up to 50 marker sorties of which at least 30 or even more would be flown over the hardest targets in Germany including the Ruhr.

It was to prove a lesson to me and now after all these years I wonder if we shall ever see their like again. It is not impossible that two world wars should drain this country of much of the spirit with which we faced the enemy in the past – the so-called permissive society with its lowered standards and neglect of the disciplines might be less willing to accept the kind of sacrifice which characterised the earlier conflicts. No doubt, a similar question was posed after the First World War but the case is no longer quite the same: the pattern of life changed greatly after 1945 and our stature has diminished in a way which barely seemed possible after the Victory Parade.

Dinghy drill on the river at the Pike and Eel – a very convenient location – was a riot of fun with plenty of ducking amid shouts of laughter. We were joined by a group of young officers from Graveley – another Pathfinder airfield nearby – led by 'Robbie' himself (Group Captain B.V. Robinson, mentioned in a previous chapter) and a dinghy race was the outcome. The weather was warm and the afternoon passed in an atmosphere of good fellowship whilst the war seemed far away.

That evening Robbie took me to Grantchester – to the Green Man – and later we walked by the river for a while. He was not one for talking much – unless the subject was rugby football – and he had seen a lot of war during the first three years: he was a regular officer and had he lived would have gone far because he had all the right attributes. He was a convinced Pathfinder and believed it was the only solution to the problem of getting bombs on the target whilst he foresaw a reduction in the casualty rate through 'swamping' the defences. He had a good squadron in No 35 and was immensely proud of their achievements though he did not put it in quite that fashion. I remember his concern for the very young crews and this is in line with the manner in which he met his death; not everyone chose to accompany a new crew on its first marking sortie but he accepted this as part of his duty as a squadron commander. I know he was a keen disciplinarian and ran his squadron according to his particular beliefs, which was his prerogative, and one was either part of the show or nothing at all in his eyes.

Duisburg, Bochum and Pilsen were attacked in that week and we lost two good crews – Flight Lieutenant Rickenson and Sergeant Renshaw – the latter having come with me from Syerston. Dortmund was laid on again for the night of 23rd May. This was a massive operation and there were sounds of indrawn breath at briefing when I announced a total of 800 taking part. It was another night to remember with clear skies over the city: the flak was heavy – accurate for height – and sent up with a speed and precision rarely equalled in my experience. How those German gunners worked!

Unlike my old Lancaster 'Y'-Yorker which had carried me so nimbly over Germany during my time with 106, the 83 Squadron aircraft seemed sluggish: our total load was 11,500 lbs of bombs and target indicators – getting on for six tons – and she clawed her way up to 18,000 feet with no heart for the business whatever. At this altitude she settled down more or less comfortably though I was far from being happy with her performance. Aircraft varied and some were certainly better than others but this old girl had a character all her own and I kept my fingers crossed, hoping we would not be caught in a searchlight cone with the need for some smart manoeuvring whilst loaded. The marking appeared well concentrated and we ran in to drop our markers on the spreading pattern of reds and greens below. The scene was a mixture of horror and incredible beauty at one and the same time: the stiff white fingers of the searchlights crossing and recrossing in their efforts to hold the stream of attackers ploughing their way across the doomed city amid a storm of bursting high explosive.

Looking down I saw the orange and red coloured smoke from the many fires, penetrated by the sullen red flickers of the bomb bursts. I was glad to pull away from that lot at the end of the bombing run and put the nose of the lethargic 'O'-Orange in a climbing turn to starboard only to encounter a perfect piece of 'bracketing' by six or eight shells from one of the super batteries which the enemy had brought in to reinforce his ground defences. Had we been at a lower altitude they would have got us but the spread of shot at 20,000 feet gave us that little bit of margin which made all the difference between a sudden exit and a return to bacon and eggs back at Wyton.

With the moon rising for the return there were many vapour trails observed creating ideal conditions for the enemy night fighters who followed them in the certainty of finding a British bomber at the issuing end. Between the Ruhr and the Dutch Coast a running battle ensued with streams of level tracer seen at varying altitudes and I had every pair of eyes watching the sky: only the taciturn John Dunk – squadron leader and navigator par excellence – stuck at his table intent on his Gee box and leaving his personal safety entirely in my hands. I saw the hostile shore line disappear behind us with the usual feeling of relief – a safe deliverance once again and we made it back to Wyton without incident. Our losses were 38 bombers – nearly 5% of the attacking force and in line with most Ruhr ventures though I deemed them heavy considering the relatively short time over enemy territory.[1] The Ruhr, the Ruhr – always the bloody Ruhr! We didn't know the Battle of the Ruhr, as it was later termed, had begun and would not have been thrilled if the Commander-in-Chief had come to Wyton and told us so. Who was he? He didn't come to see us and yet he held us in the palm of his hand day after day – or rather night after night? 'The Butcher' made his presence felt though and we all twitched when he pulled the string.

Dortmund must have pleased him – it was a most successful and damaging onslaught – pulled off for him by a row of ex-bank clerks, school teachers, farmers and one aspiring candidate for Holy Orders who, alas, never made it. I can assure the gentle reader that the bomber crews were no whit different from other men and inclined to vent their feelings every now and again. Bennett we knew – he was our immediate chief and, of course, we had the customary flow of 'visiting firemen' from all kinds of high offices. Lord Wavell, was in a quite different category – I had the honour to lunch at the same table when he came to Wyton on 4th June and never uttered a word concerning himself but was quick to recognise the assistance provided by a 106 Squadron Lancaster which flew him back from North Africa. This was during the time I had the squadron and he flew with Sergeant Page, a capable young NCO pilot who, having lost an engine over La Spezia, very sensibly carried on to North Africa and landed at Maison Blanche. This was most opportune for the Field Marshal who was stuck for a ride home and the last thing he expected to see was a limping Lancaster fly over the desert to his aid. Anyway, Wavell was splendid and oozed greatness.

The reactions of the crews to visits from ministers, members of the Air Council and so forth was not much – and this is hardly surprising. Sometimes at briefing they saw our AOC arrive with some important individual who would exchange a few words with the pilots and navigators afterwards, walking among them in friendly fashion and expressing interest in their task.

What the Minister of Something or Other thought about the squadron didn't matter a hoot to men about to risk their necks over the enemy's country but it did perhaps matter to officers higher up in the scale. Their future might well be affected by the impression gained by someone like the Inspector General – a powerful individual to whom all doors were open anywhere in the Royal Air Force though he would scarcely intrude in operational matters. A few daft questions might be asked by someone outside the Royal Air Force and I recall one irritating gentleman enquiring of Frank Forster – Flight Lieutenant, Royal Australian Air Force and my flight engineer – whether the particular target announced at briefing was likely to produce more casualties than any similar objective. I saw the glint in Frank's eye and whipped the questioner away before he was exposed to a curt and dusty response, though afterwards I wished I had left him to his fate.

In general Bennett protected us from idiots and was cautious as to whom he brought to the briefing room. However, and on a lighter note, a one-time famous American film actor appeared on the station, making a courtesy visit in his role as a Special Representative: in fact he wore a brown battle dress with a suitable shoulder flash making it all official. On that day 'Robbie' was acting station commander and invited me to lunch with them at his table. The Famous Actor was very entertaining and lacked nothing in self-confidence: charming was the better word and he certainly earned his lunch. He meant well and shook us warmly by the hand after getting up from table, paused for a moment, then dived into an inside pocket to produce large signed photographs of himself. This was kind, and I still retain the glossy image of that famous face.

On one occasion I travelled from Huntingdon to King's Cross with another celebrity but he was cast in a very different mould – Captain Clark Gable – who flew with the American 351st Bomb Group. He was friendly and spoke of everything except himself, expressing his admiration for the Royal Air Force and Bomber Command in particular. A fat Rolls was waiting for him at the terminus and he offered me a lift to anywhere in London but I had made other arrangements and we parted after a handshake. He was all right – I could get along with him.

Bennett, by virtue of his reputation and the position he occupied drew many important people to his Pathfinder Headquarters and he invariably invited one or other of his squadron commanders of staff along to his house for drinks or dinner. He was a good host and though a total abstainer himself never sought to convert others: his parties were quite delightful and we played old fashioned games like charades and similar antics with enthusiasm. Relaxed and easy in manner he did much to draw us all together.

And so back to the Ruhr once again – to Wuppertal on the night of 29th May, a town lying on the eastern side of the Ruhr Valley and attacked from the south-west after by-passing Cologne and Düsseldorf. At least that was the idea but in fact it proved a 'gauntlet' effort, mile after mile of bursting shells, and over the target we encountered the toughest barrage fire ever. The crack of the flak burst and the continuous procession of black puffs which marked our passage brought home the solemn prophecy that 'Man has but a short time to live and is full of misery ...' We were not hit but our bombsight threw a fault as we were settling down to a steady run up to the red.*Oboe* marker dropped by the 109 Squadron Mosquito and I decided not to release the green back-up indicators which we carried in the bomb bay. The high explosive we sent down as a matter of course and it landed somewhere in the vicinity but the dropping of the vital marker bombs was cancelled: the risk of misleading the main force of heavies thundering along behind us could not be accepted. It was maddening after all the preparation and hours of getting steamed up for the fray and it might have been better to have washed out the sortie rather than have this miserable result to report on our return.

I counted five bombers going down in flames between leaving the Ruhr and seeing the coast once more whilst our total losses for the night were 33 bombers with a further 71 damaged. These figures compared with the Dortmund raid since 700 heavies went into the attack. Thus, a pattern was beginning to shape and on clear nights with no cloud cover this was what we could expect. The comfort of a thousand feet thick cloud layer may not be overestimated – something to duck into with the enemy on one's tail – always providing he was spotted in time. The long 'stalk' from way back using airborne radar on a dark night was another matter entirely.

To fly a marshal or a general on a 'look see' over the Ruhr was always my ambition and I came very near realising it later when two brass hats arrived from Whitehall – both Americans and anxious to acquire a bit of local colour. They attended my briefing and made their request – which was vetoed by the RAF officer in charge of the party. I was all for it and pleaded with him to let these keen general officers have their money's worth but he waved a bit of paper at me saying such a move was not in the official programme. I think he was scared of failing to return them in one piece to the London headquarters and seemed very agitated when I assured both generals, 'It's no trouble at all – we'd love to have you along.'

The taller general looked at me shrewdly: 'Why so keen, son, and what's so special about the Ruhr?'

'You'll find it well worthwhile, sir; every senior officer should make a trip or two. I guarantee you won't be disappointed.'

He laughed. 'OK – that's a deal. Leave the arrangements to me – I'll fix it with your people.' He was as good as his word and accompanied Flight Lieutenant Garvey to the Ruhr – Essen in fact. This was General Fred Anderson and he and I dined with Bennett before take-off. He was pleased with the treatment and returned one day with gifts for the crew – a nice gesture, from a thoroughly nice man.[2] There was no ceremony with these Americans – they attached no importance to their choice of a Ruhr target and it appears that generals of the United States Army Air Force were expendable! Later when the huge formations of Fortresses and Liberators became a daily spectacle in the skies of East Anglia the 'Lead Ship' invariably carried a general officer. And how we liked that one! Granted, we did not fly in tight formations like the Americans, but it might have been no bad thing for our own group commanders to have put in the odd sortie – always excluding the gallant Embry – Air Chief Marshal eventually, and one of the best – who flew steadily in the face of a direct order not to do so. There were others, of course, but at one stage we were the only group to boast an Air Officer Commanding – Donald Bennett – who had been through the hoop in our war. Later, John Whitley and Hugh Constantine, both exceptionally well qualified operationally succeeded to the command of bomber groups.[3]

The results of the Wuppertal attack astonished everybody – it proved the most accurate to date and this despite the few red *Oboe* markers observed. The precision with which the Backers-Up seized upon the early marking by the first Mosquito flying at 30,000 feet was the key to success because owing to equipment failure in the Mosquitos the aiming point was not freshly marked for another eighteen minutes by a second radar directed indicator. Had we chanced it with our own bombsight we might well have spoiled the show. Poor Robbie had bad luck losing four of his best crews on the night: 35 Squadron took a real beating and we were very sad on this score – to lose four good Pathfinder crews was a severe blow.

NOTES

1. This raid on Dortmund, on the night of 23/24th May 1943, was carried out by 826 bombers, the largest force dispatched since the specially collected 'Thousand Bomber Raids' of 1942. The Dortmund raid was very successful, the most destructive of the Battle of the Ruhr period.

2. This was Brigadier-General Frederick L. Anderson, the new commander of VIII Bomber Command, the heavy bomber force in the US Eight Air Force. Flight Lieutenant 'Ricky' Garvey, a Canadian pilot on Searby's squadron, not only took Anderson to Essen but also to Hamburg two nights later (the nights of 25/26th and 27/28th July 1943), the latter being the night of the Hamburg Firestorm. The Lancaster in which these flights were made was the famous R 5868 which later completed 137

operational flights and is now on permanent display at the RAF Museum at Hendon. Anderson survived the war, but not Garvey who was killed in a crash while flying an Oxford in England later in the war.

3. There was a general reshuffle of group commanders towards the end of the war in which experienced operational officers like Air Vice-Marshals J.R. Whitley and H.A. Constantine were given the opportunity to hold command positions before the war in Europe ended.

CHAPTER SIX

'How many more lives?'

Following the Wuppertal operation, a long spell of bad weather brought a series of cancellations: targets were laid on and cancelled with sickening monotony, though we went through all the motions right up to a few minutes before take-off more than once. The men who suffered most were the armament staffs who fused and hauled the 'cookies', 1,000-pounders and incendiary bomb containers to the dispersal pans, winching them up to the bomb hooks only to remove them an hour later. Whilst we possessed the means of marking a Ruhr target with an accuracy previously believed impossible, we could not defeat the weather. 'Sky marking', whereby coloured flares were released over the objective on a signal from the ground radar control enabled us to bomb through thick cloud, but this technique was of little use if the raiding force could not be landed back safely. Low cloud and heavy rain marked the first ten days of June and it became something of a problem to keep the aircrew occupied. Lectures, discussions and 'dry swims', the last being an exercise on the plotting chart, were relieved by a visit to the Leys School at Cambridge where dinghy drill was practised in the covered swimming pool, but the boredom was damaging. 'Man proposes ...' The Met Staff shrugged their shoulders and could offer no prospect of relief from the perpetual wetness which seemed to be our lot. The hangar floors ran with moisture and and the ground maintenance fitters, normally• flush with work, stood around in groups with idle hands. Then someone came along with the idea that a 'Station Defence Exercise' might be a sound solution whilst contributing something to security at the same time.

No half measures, everyone was drawn in including the aircrew and the local RAF Regiment commander; sten guns, rifles and revolvers were issued: a selected band of aircrew were given the task of penetrating the station defences at various points and in the beginning there was certain enthusiasm evident. It lasted two days and we all got soaked: the defences proved more than adequate and authority was satisfied. The bedraggled air gunners, navigators and pilots captured on the perimeter voted the experience far worse than a Ruhr sortie and bent to the monotonous work in the simulators with fresh energy – no one wanted a repeat performance. Our flight sergeant, a veteran of the '14-'18 war with a long record of service in the Royal Air Force, was the only man to remain warm and dry throughout, ensconced in his comfortable hut out on the dispersal area from which he refused to budge in his capacity as umpire. As an old soldier he knew the form.

The squadron photograph taken around that time is impressive though marred somewhat by the black crosses – killed in action, but not forgotten. The front row in the group are all squadron leaders: Chisholm, Scrivener, Burt, Smith and the two Johnsons, another Smith, John Manton and Archie Cochrane, whilst standing behind are the other officers. Pretty well everyone is smiling – youth at its brightest and best. A few are absent through leave and other reasons.

Guy Sells is not in the picture – another squadron leader – and it is not unlikely he chose to remain anonymous. He had little use for publicity or any kind of show but was a first class captain and one of the keenest Pathfinders, surviving heaven knows how many sorties over Germany. A grunt was his only acknowledgement that he was in the Battle Order for the night and he could never be drawn out save on the subject of cricket at which he was no mean performer with the bat. He had studied at Munich before the war and during the wet spell when we filled in time with talks on various subjects he was persuaded to speak about life in the Bavarian capital and the habits of the German professors. This proved a diverting interlude. Guy treated the war as an incident only, doing all he was asked to do with quiet efficiency, and was without doubt one of the most successful Pathfinder captains to serve under Bennett.

In the old photograph are some 40 officers and no less than 20 are wearing the ribbon of the Distinguished Flying Cross or Medal Norman Hildyard and Harry Shaw had 'A' and 'B' Flights when I took over and each completed his tour in a matter of a few weeks to be replaced by Ambrose Smith and John Manton – the former being an ex-Oxford University Air Squadron member and Manton a 'Regular'. Ambrose more than did his duty by his constant place in the battle order – experienced, steady as a rock and highly respected: he ran his flight with a light but very firm hand and his judgement was sound, but he wasn't a 'career' officer; seeking only to do his job and return to university one day. I believe he would have gone far had he stayed in the service.

John Manton had volunteered for the Pathfinder Force on his return from India, to his great credit, and his crew was special to me in that somewhere along the way he had collected Archie Cochrane, an old friend of many years standing, and a squadron leader/navigator. They flew fifteen sorties together with great success right up to the time of the Leipzig attack in October 1943 – undertaken on a night of storm and strong winds which turned the operation into a shambles. They never returned, to my great grief. That night we lost two aircraft – Manton and Warrant Officer Hall and on the return my aircraft were badly scattered. Two more were badly shot up by a night fighter but struggled back across the North Sea – one pulling off an incredible landing with three engines feathered on the approach and bomb doors falling away as he landed – to which the complete absence of any brake pressure contributed an extra hazard.

I remained in Flying Control until it was clear the aircraft would not return and after snatching a couple of hours' sleep collected all Archie's gear from the room he occupied in the mess and drove to Cambridge where his family lived. It was just after 7 a.m. when I found the house and broke the news to his wife who bore up bravely but it was an unhappy mission which I have never forgotten. He was a gentle person possessed of a certain stubbornness – gifted and a good musician – lacking nothing in cold courage and unwilling to take any kind of advantage of anybody.[1]

The small figure in the front row is that of my own navigator – Norman Scrivener. His record of sorties is formidable, notching over a hundred plus at the time he finished his Pathfinder tour of duty. When the going was rough, he carried on methodically ignoring the noises outside the aircraft and ready instantly with a new course after the kerfuffle was over. He never flapped. 'Captain to Navigator – how much longer to the French coast?' A prolonged silence, then, 'Navigator answering – 32 minutes – and seven since the last request for information.' This was an indication of his displeasure at the interruption to his calculations: he gave precise information at regular intervals and I had been guilty of a procedural error! I collected him on one particular evening from the Golden Lion at St Ives when he had climbed on to the bar and offered to take on all comers. In that small frame lay an indomitable spirit – my own personal debt to Norman Scrivener is more than I can ever hope to repay.

'Smithy' – more correctly Squadron Leader C.A.G. Smith DSO, DFC, sits between John Manton and Norman Burt. He is still flourishing; imperturbable, good-humoured and a top rate pianist, he was the arch type of Pathfinder captain – returning so many times with a battered aircraft after marking the way for others to follow: he bore a charmed life. 'Johnny', our gunnery leader, devoted the rest of his life to looking after others when he left the Service and there is no higher praise.

Squadron Leader Blair, mentioned earlier is not shown. He flew with Smithy – a happy combination and unique in some ways for their characters differed widely but they always brought home the bacon and were usually first in on the tough targets. Where do the Blairs of this world come from? One wishes there were more of them in these unsettled times; as warriors they have left their mark, leading the 'forlorn hope' and cheering on the faint-hearted; hard fighters, boisterous promoters of the off-duty get-together and loyal to the last. Surviving many scrapes, he remained the plain English gentleman, observing that the ship was more important than the crew and silencing any criticism of authority with a blast which sent the blood to their boots. The men were proud of Tommy and the women adored him, but he was quite unaffected. He got into scrapes and charmed his way out of them to survive the war with a DSO and DFC – not one whit changed by his experiences. Alas, he is no longer with us.

Bomber Command drew the best. The 'Dull Boys' as one senior officer called them performed a dull task – a slogging match with no highlights – or very few – and that was how it was. They were never sparing of praise for the deeds of others – those isolated, single acts of gallantry for which this nation is justly famous – but acted out their part as circumstances required.

With improved weather conditions the offensive was renewed: we lost Squadron Leader Swift and his crew over Münster on 11th June and Flying Officer Tilbury the following night over Bochum. The latter had volunteered for Pathfinder duty the previous March from 106 and I knew him and his crew well. Both these attacks were part of the Battle of the Ruhr which was growing in intensity and which, stemming from the extraordinary accuracy of the *Oboe* Mosquito marking, was laying great areas of the most important cities in ruins. Düsseldorf had been attacked along with Münster and, in the words of the Official History, had the heart torn out of it. One hundred and thirty acres of Bochum were laid waste only 24 hours later. Flying Officer Tilbury captained a special team of radar operators – expert on the use of the airborne radar system H_2S – and his loss was important to the success of our future operations. He was a fine youngster – a competent captain, steady and sure in all he undertook and had he remained with his first squadron, 106, would have completed his tour of duty – safely. Yet he volunteered for more dangerous work and is remembered by those who knew him.[2]

An unusual feature of that particular week in June was the display of Northern Lights which, coupled with a bright moon, undoubtedly added to our losses. The spread of light to the north of us, streams of great beauty at times, resulted in a background against which we were starkly defined. We celebrated the award of the Conspicuous Gallantry Medal to Pilot Officer Preece – my rear gunner who had been awarded the Distinguished Flying Medal some time before – and Frank Forster, the flight engineer, pulled off a 'double' with a commission and a DFC in the same breath. Ross, our bomb aimer, collected a DFM which was well deserved, though a quieter individual it would have been hard to find – or so I thought until I happened to overhear him conveying his thoughts to a newly joined crew one noontime. It was a pure accident and I pretended not to have heard a word. As I entered the ante room he was going through the motions, in an exaggerated manner, of a pilot at the controls of a bomber – and breathing heavily whilst pretending to wipe the sweat from his brow with the other hand. 'There you are, chaps. That's Honest John on the bombing run!' When he turned and saw me standing quite near he went several shades of crimson – but I never let on that I had heard a word and he never knew for sure. As to whom 'Honest John' might be, I leave the reader to guess.

Ross was a fine character and his death over Berlin on 20th January the following year affected me greatly. When I handed over 83 Squadron he had completed 45 sorties but elected to continue until he had flown the Pathfinder complement of a full 60. He joined up with a young Australian captain – Flying Officer R. King – and they were among the 34 lost over the 'Big City' that night. We had survived many a close call during the time I had 106 and later in the Pathfinder Force: he was very young like most of his fellows – courageous and cool under fire – and his shy humour gained him many friends.[3]

A few days later we had a break in the Ruhr business and Le Creusot – the French armament factory making guns for the German Army since the occupation – came up for attention.

Le Creusot evokes memories of Guy Gibson. He led 106 in the daylight swoop on the armament works in October '42 and I recall his enthusiasm when the target was announced. The 90 Lancasters led by Group Captain L.C. Slee had attacked at low level with but one casualty: a unique experience and rare in the list of 'daylights' forced home by low-flying 'heavies' of Bomber Command. The second attack, on 19th June 1943, took place by night and was only moderately successful. My own squadron was directed to destroy the switching station at Montchanin, a few miles to the south, which supplied power to the armament factory after first illuminating the site with the magnesium flares we carried. Since it was lightly defended, the attack went in at 5,000 feet after a low approach down the Loire Valley. I had my usual crew – Norman Scrivener, Frank Forster, George Ross, Leslie Davies with George Coley and Preece in the gun turrets. Coley was to fly with me on successive operations for the rest of my time with 83: he was a character and very popular since he excelled at the customary indoor sports and could carry a remarkable quantity of beer without obvious effect. This was not the reason for my selecting him – he had other and more useful talents as a gunner and was recommended by 'Johnny', our gunnery leader, a man not given to praising his men without very good reason. So Coley joined us and in the event lived up to his name.

There was a full moon that night and having arrived at the Loire we flew over picture-book country. At one point I let down to 1500 feet and we took in the spectacle of wooded hills, quiet farms and sparkling châteaux clearly visible in the white moonlight. The great river with its many channels, islands and sand banks flowed peacefully reflecting the staring moon and it all seemed far removed from the war and the nightly horrors to which we had become inured. The French people, knowing these were British bombers, flung open their doors and we saw lights flashing below – friendly lights, unlike the darting red and green incendiary shells from the muzzles of the 20mm light flak batteries

– conveying a welcome and the good wishes of a people sick of the German occupation.

We found Montchanin without difficulty and the attack on the main target began in the same moment: I saw the flares float down laying bare the country around the factory; hanging over the target with brilliant effect. Ross lying in the nose was ecstatic: never had such an opportunity been offered to him and he was not content with one or even two runs before he had his sights properly aligned. We dropped on the fifth at 4,500 feet over the massive array of steel masts, condensers and switching houses. Three 1,000-pounders and eight 500-pounders fell squarely into the middle with bright blue flashes prominent among the bursts. Our night camera was turning over and when the film was developed next morning Ross had secured a fine aiming point picture – the point of impact of his bombs lying squarely in the centre. Admittedly, this was small stuff – an easy target with only a few light flak guns to defend it – but it was worthwhile and the recce aircraft confirmed the damage the following day.[4] Dawn was breaking as we left the French coast behind, landing at Wyton as the sun rose. The very short nights of mid-summer precluded deep penetrations of Occupied Europe though there were exceptions when we made our escape out over the French Atlantic coast, making a long haul back round the Brest Peninsula.

By way of a change I went back to Syerston on the Sunday, when we were stood down from operating, to attend the Wings for Victory Service in Southwell Cathedral. My successor in 106 Squadron read one lesson and I read the other – the Parable of the Good Samaritan. 'Oddie' – Group Captain Odbert, the station commander, had invited me and I was glad to renew acquaintance with my old squadron once more. We were all thrilled by the rendering of Purcell's 'Trumpet Voluntary' on the cathedral organ, accompanied by a solitary trumpeter wearing the uniform of the National Fire Service. The scene was one of colour and even brilliance: all the fighting services were represented, the nurses, Civil Defence, firemen, Home Guard. It was one of those moments easily recalled over the years. At the mess I lunched with 'Oddie' and Ronnie Baxter then flew back to Wyton only to return a month later for the former's funeral: he was killed in a flying accident whilst occupying the rear turret of a Wellington and is buried at Newark. Although I knew him for only a short time I remember him as one of the kindest and most honourable men I had the good fortune to serve.

Krefeld in the Ruhr cost us 44 bombers the following day, out of a total of 700 dispatched; we lost two from 83 – Pilot Officer Mappin and Flight Sergeant Fletcher – and 35 Squadron lost no less than six Halifaxes. The early markers were literally hacked down by flak and hordes of night fighters. 'Robbie' Robinson at Graveley was desolated – it was his station that took this phenomenal beating and he was in a black mood. He attributed his losses to the increased night-fighter strength but I think it was one occasion when the first Pathfinders going in to back up the Mosquito marking caught the blast of more than a hundred heavy anti-aircraft guns firing a long box barrage dead in the path of the bombers. This had happened previously over Cologne when a few Pathfinders – ahead of the main bombing force – were swamped by the concentrated fire of the ground defences. The damned Ruhr – how many more lives would it claim – how many more crews would be lost over those grim cities along the Rhine? 'Many thousands' was to be the ultimate count – and this was early days.[5]

With the turn of the year things would be far worse and it was just as well we had no crystal ball. Half of my squadron had disappeared in the past eleven days – all good crews – and replacement wasn't easy. Our dependence on volunteers from the Main Force Groups was a critical factor in keeping squadrons up to strength and a time was drawing near when this, the best of all methods, would fail. 'Pressed men' are as nothing beside a volunteer and the nearest we could get to the latter at one stage was a crew posted willy-nilly by a Group Headquarters with a genuine regard for the problems of the PFF.

The difficulty of obtaining above-average crews possessing a good record of successful sorties was tackled by one of Bennett's staff officers – Wing Commander T.G. Mahaddie DSO, DFC, AFC – who stumped the group territories seeking such men. He was successful and it was a thankless task at times – one needed a smooth tongue and a thick skin: the prejudices of station and squadron commanders had to be overcome – if present, which was not always the case but was not unknown. No squadron commander drew satisfaction from being relieved of his best men and sometimes a compromise was reached whereby a substitute was put up – a certain amount of haggling might take place so that the term 'horse-dealing' gained acceptance. Hamish Mahaddie displayed a unique talent for the job and became a familiar figure in the briefing rooms and messes of the many bomber stations. His own fine record was a passport to most places whilst his personality was such that he made few enemies in the pursuit of the best for the PFF. He kept us going though it was becoming obvious that the longer the war dragged on the more difficult his task. There were other problems, too.

An increasing independence, deriving from a policy which permitted Nos 5 and 3 Groups to operate parallel to the remainder of the Bomber Command on occasions, diminished the flow of battle-hardened crews and our AOC – Don Bennett – spoke to me about the possibility of taking pilots and navigators possessing little more than basic training at the Flying and Navigation Training establishments directly into his own Pathfinder Group. This actually happened in the case of two or three young pilots arriving at Wyton who were thrust into the driving seat of a Lancaster for the first time. The experiment was successful, as I remember and, despite the lack of intermediate training, they adapted quickly to the aircraft and the scheme could have worked very well since we had our own Training Unit at Warboys.

This establishment had been formed to groom officers for the special duties of marking targets and a like facility extended to the navigators: it all began with a conviction on Bennett's part that the standards observed in certain quarters fell below his own: the narrow margins demanded in track keeping and timing, the careful training in the operation of the H_2S radar for identifying ground features and targets could best be in a Pathfinder environment under his own control, and, therefore all crews joining his squadrons must go through the Warboys' curriculum en route.

The need for utter reliability and accuracy when placing the target indicators requires no emphasis – with several hundred bombers converging on an objective a single stray marker bomb could neutralise a large slice of the attacking potential – whilst the vast amount of labour expended in preparation coupled with the possibility of losing valuable lives and aircraft unnecessarily called for the strictest supervision: he was determined that mistakes should be few – if any at all. That errors were made by the Pathfinders is not disputed but they were remarkably few in number when the duration and magnitude of the task is taken into consideration.

The control of a big attack led by a marking force is, quite obviously, more difficult than the control for a small one: there is more room for the multiplication of error as the attack progresses and the introduction of a Master Bomber was calculated to reduce such errors. The precision later achieved during the independent 5 Group operations demonstrates both points: tight control of the hundred plus bombers by radio made possible the recentring of the bombing pattern and enabled the attack to be called off briefly to enable fresh marking to be done. This was never possible with 800 bombers flying in strictly timed waves and briefed to be over the target inside a narrow time-band: once the big attack was rolling nothing could stop it and despite the presence of a Master Bomber it became a patching-up process on those occasions when attacks were made outside the range of *Oboe*, and it should be noted that in all the big attacks carried out at long range the Pathfinder Force bore the responsibility. The Ruhr attacks were essentially a Pathfinder show since the Mosquitos of 109 Squadron were part of Bennett's 8 Group.

All in all Bennett had many headaches and his constant effort to improve the marking on the far-flung targets made for many trials and discussions. He had great faith in the airborne radar H_2S and as time went by we improved greatly though we could never hope for the kind of results possible with the ground-monitored *Oboe*. The *Newhaven* method evolved by him was the best in the circumstances, embracing the use of the radar and the employment of visual markers – selected for their reliability and determination to press home the attack.

The lot of the bomber navigator was never a happy one and at times he must have felt like throwing his hand in during the very early period of the war. As indicated earlier, great strides were made in 1942 and by the middle of the following year he was equipped with just about everything from radar to the equipment which recorded automatically his air position – the Air Position Indicator – and yet he still had his moments. Noise, cold, enemy action and weather were always factors for error whilst unserviceability of the 'black boxes' could throw him back to basic methods.

'Keep the Air Plot going' was a favourite phrase – which, quite simply, meant maintaining course and air speed on the chart for the whole time he was in the air. This was, indeed, a golden rule and rarely broken. Each navigator worked to his own satisfaction using all available aids and careful planning before flight was the beginning of success in the air: confidence grew with successive sorties as the crew worked up but none could share his responsibility – the position, course and time to the next turning point belonged uniquely to the navigator. The captain had responsibility for all but he was entirely dependent on his navigator who alone could get him to the target and home again. There was no question of the captain leaving his seat to monitor the work done on the chart – he wasn't trained for it, save in exceptional circumstances, and his knowledge did not extend beyond the limits of 'Air Pilotage' – and once over enemy territory it would not have made sense.

It was usual to work to the limit of *Gee* range which guaranteed a fair accuracy depending on conditions; after that the navigator would work on dead reckoning, supplemented by every possible scrap of useful information such as 'pin-points' from the bomb aimer peering down from the nose and, if the aircraft was so equipped, he would switch on his H_2S which would reproduce coast lines, cities and in fact anything capable of reflecting the transmission from the rotating scanner attached to the belly of the bomber. The bubble sextant was rarely used after 1942 but over the North Sea I have taken a sight from the pilot's seat with my navigator holding the deck watch and recording the time of observation: this may not have been the perfect answer but it worked very well.

The invasion of Sicily which began during the second week in July prompted more bomber attacks on Northern Italy with the aim of interrupting supplies to the German and Italian units fighting in Sicily. There was no shortage of volunteers for a ride over the Alps after the Ruhr battles and in the earlier attacks we had usually got away with hardly a scratch. Thus we were surprised to lose no less than thirteen bombers on the night of 12th July, though it is possible some of these were shot down off the Brest Peninsula on the way home.[6] This long and circuitous route was necessary since the hours of darkness were short and had we returned over the direct route we might have been caught by German fighters in broad daylight. There was one highlight for my own crew: we were within an ace of colliding with a Halifax over Lake Annecy on the way in – it was the nearest thing ever and far too close for comfort. He literally brushed us with his tail plane. Off Brest we encountered Ju88s and I was down to a few feet over the water forty miles out into the Atlantic as we doubled the peninsula and made for the safety of the English Channel.

It was a perfect morning with the sun shining on the wavetops but we were heavily fatigued after ten hours and glad to get home. How those thirteen bombers were lost I shall always wonder because we saw no one hit over Turin and they must have fallen victims to the Ju88s intercepting us off Brest. A few nights later we went to Hamburg for the opening of the battle which was to lay that proud city flatter than a billiard table and produce the greatest fire-storm of the war in Europe.

NOTES

1. The crews of Squadron Leader R.J. Manton and Warrant Officer S.G. Hall were all killed. Manton's Lancaster was shot down by a night fighter and the crew, including John Searby's friend, Archie Cochrane, are the only British servicemen buried in a civilian cemetery at the Dutch town of Assen. No trace was ever found of Warrant Officer Hall's crew and it is assumed that they were shot down into the sea.

2. Flying Officer E.A. Tilbury's crew were also killed when their Lancaster was shot down over Holland, crashing into the Ijselmeer. Tilbury and three others are buried in various local cemeteries; the other three men have no known grave.

3. Flight Lieutenant W.G. Ross, DFC, DFM, and five other members of (then) Flight Lieutenant King's crew died when their Lancaster was hit by flak over Berlin and they are buried in the Berlin War Cemetery. Flight Lieutenant King survived as a prisoner of war; Lancaster pilots were sometimes fortunate to be thrown clear when their aircraft blew up, due to the construction of the aircraft often producing a clean break at the pilot's position.

4. The attack by the small force of bombers on the electrical-transformer station at Montchanin was actually a failure, most of the aircraft involved mistaking a nearby small factory for the true target. Only a few aircraft identified the real target and no hits were scored on it.

5. The Krefeld raid – on the night of 21/22nd June 1943 – did, as Searby says, cause heavy casualties to the Pathfinders, twelve of their aircraft being among the 44 aircraft lost that night from the 705 taking part in the raid. But the raid on this industrial target was particularly effective and was probably the most damaging raid carried out by Bomber Command thus far in the war.

The two 83 Squadron crews – of Pilot Officer H. Mappin and Flight Sergeant D.W.C. Fletcher – all perished when shot down, Fletcher's over Holland and Mappin's in the sea just off the Dutch Frisian Islands.

6. Among the casualties on this night was Wing Commander J.D. Nettleton, who, on 17th April 1942, won a Victoria Cross leading the daylight attack on Augsburg. Nettleton's Lancaster was probably shot down into the sea off Brittany on the return flight; there were no survivors in his crew. His name is on the Runnymede Memorial to the Missing.

CHAPTER SEVEN

Hamburg

By the late summer of 1943 Bomber Command was expanding rapidly: a marked increase in the numbers of four-engined aircraft enabled the Commander-in-Chief to commit some 700 bombers to battle and these included a significant total of Lancasters. Eventually, a massive force of 1,600 heavy bombers would be available for operations but that did not happen until the final year of the conflict. If we take a figure of 800 'heavies' this represents the strength at the time of the Ruhr, Hamburg and Berlin battles which took place in the spring, summer and autumn of 1943. The Stirlings and Wellingtons were replaced by Lancasters in that year and the bomb tonnage greatly increased thereby. The advance in radar techniques was striking as the year passed whilst the operations of No 100 Group, created to exploit the use of radio counter-measures in support of our attacks, is noteworthy. All these improvements and additions to our armoury worked to one end – that of striking the enemy down at the lowest cost in lives and aircraft. The face of Bomber Command was changing and new elements were appearing: new minds, new tactics and occasional differences between people, between the Main Force groups and the Pathfinder Force, which lost some of the backing to which it was entitled, bearing in mind the conditions and circumstances which attended its formation.

In his first volume of the Official History,* Dr Noble Frankland has adduced the arguments surrounding the establishment of the Pathfinder Force with great clarity: himself a bomber navigator with a full quota of sorties to his credit, he is uniquely qualified to record a situation where Bennett, through no fault of his own, occupied a central position among older and more senior officers whose authority had been exercised from the outbreak of the war. By implication Pathfinder crews were to be picked men of proved reliability and determination and it follows that the officer elected

* *The Strategic Air Offensive against Germany 1939-1945* (3 vols) C. Webster and N. Frankland, HMSO 1961.

to lead such a force should at least match the qualifications of his captains. On the basis of an earlier relationship, and Bennett's record since that time, Sir Arthur Harris chose him for what some might think to be an unenviable task – the tactical leadership of the whole bomber force. By that token Bennett was entitled to expect the full support of his Commander-in-Chief come wind or weather. It did not happen quite like that and a situation was to arise where the Main Force groups 'tended to compete rather than co-operate with the Pathfinder Force' though it should be noted that every big raid, every 'blood and guts' target continued to fall into Bennett's orbit since only the Pathfinders were geared to the rhythmic sequence which conducted 800 heavy bombers through a stoutly defended target area such as Essen, Hamburg or Berlin. That differences of opinion should arise between commanders is not remarkable: the great Sir Basil Embry, whose gallantry and skill have passed into legend, had his doubts concerning our methods and spoke his mind freely that evening at Mongewell Park in 1944: Embry was all for using Lancasters at low level with himself in the first bomber to open the attack and I shuddered once again at the prospect, first suggested by Guy Gibson, when he showed me his low-level bombsight at Syerston! A somewhat cooler appraisal of the marking problem later came from Air Vice-Marshal Cochrane, raiser of 617 Squadron successes and an innovator of unusual ability.[1]

To go back a little: The Lancaster bomber was more than a mere aeroplane; it was the realisation of a dream which threw back a horizon previously limited by the slower and more cumbrous aircraft associated with the early days of the offensive. The jerk to morale stemming from the range, flexibility and power of this superb bomber induced confidence and superiority in those crews fortunate enough to fly it. No 5 Group, under the command of Air Vice-Marshal Alec Coryton, had fully equipped with Lancasters by the autumn of 1942 and Coryton had not been slow to appreciate the potential of the weapon under his hand. When he interviewed me for the appointment of flight commander in Gibson's squadron, he was clear and forthright as to the possibilities. Even then, I believe he saw his group destined for a special role and the execution of unusual tasks which may account for his rejection of the idea of a Pathfinder Force at the time the matter had been first debated. If there was to be an élite corps then it should be No 5 Group under his direction. He did not say this, but I am convinced this was his belief. Alec Coryton was a first rate group commander, knowledgeable, thrusting and capable of inspiring his crews so that the atmosphere of his Grantham headquarters was lively and forward-looking. Like all the 'barons' he was very much master in his own house – and maybe a bit more so than some – so that the rumoured clash with Sir Arthur Harris over the dispatch of a small force to Berlin in rough weather caused no great surprise out on the tarmac. We had all been sorry to see him go. That he should be succeeded by an officer even more convinced of the special role was an act of fate and from then on the die was cast. Coryton's replacement, Air Vice-Marshal Hon Ralph Cochrane, who had come up in the right manner, had served under Harris as a flight commander and was strongly favoured by his C-in-C. With these qualifications he was unlikely to accept second place in the hierarchy of group commanders. He made his debut with a sparkling success, using a single squadron created for the purpose of bombing the German dams and never looked back: the rapier was to challenge the bludgeon and Cochrane believed he was the man to wield it. The courage, devotion and heavy sacrifice of 617 Squadron on that memorable occasion paved the way, and the breaching of the Möhne Dam was a matter of pride among the many thousands of aircrew who formed the vast bulk of Bomber Command.

Whilst the notion of a corps d'élite was objectionable to Sir Arthur and his group commanders at the time of the forming of the Pathfinder Force, no one cavilled at Cochrane's resurrecting it. Only the best and most experienced crews were deemed fit for 617 and no effort was spared to maintain it at the highest pitch of efficiency.

The 'Marthas' who flogged their bombers to the run-of-mill targets in Germany knew their own efforts were in no wise diminished thereby and wished 617 well and, though the difference which grew up with the attempted extension of No 5 Group thinking into Bennett's territory – marking techniques – were common knowledge, they made small impact in some quarters. If a rift existed at a higher level that was one thing; whilst the daily conduct of the war, demanding the utmost from great numbers of pilots, navigators and the like, was another. One's loyalty goes to one's immediate commander and the job goes forward. A commander-in-chief is entitled to dispose of his strength in whatever fashion he believes will best achieve the aim and Sir Arthur Harris certainly favoured Cochrane. Nevertheless, the dispatch of second rate crews to Bennett to offset Pathfinder casualties, when the task and agreement demanded nothing less than the very best, was cause for anxiety and a lesser man than Bennett might well have asked to be relieved. I speak from first hand knowledge in the matter of aircrew replacements arriving from the Main Force groups and it is to Bennett's credit that he took them and made them into Pathfinders, even the reluctant ones, and there were a few of those from time to time.

To hold the ring between two such brilliant group commanders as Cochrane and Bennett must have been no easy task for Sir Arthur Harris whilst the prospect of Cochrane pulling off a series of small but highly successful attacks, equipped with the finest crews and the latest in air-to-air voice communication radio, was, no doubt, galling to a man endeavouring to carry out his brief of marking the routine objectives for the Main Force bombers following up his Pathfinder crews. Simple men would argue the case for joining forces, but it never happened in any real degree and on occasions it was not unknown for Cochrane's group to act independently within the overall framework of a heavy attack. At squadron level we humbler individuals came to accept the situation, content with our master and in no wise envious of what was done by 5 Group; we had our own problems. Later, I served Sir Ralph Cochrane at Headquarters Transport Command and he was very kind to me: I found him able, incisive and very human.

On 24th July the Battle of Hamburg began. The previous evening there was a small party in the mess interrupted by a telephone call from some kind soul in St Ives – about forty miles away – to say that a member of my squadron had run amok in the Golden Lion Hotel and would I arrange for him to be collected before the local Police came. I tore off to get him and found a very young officer somewhat the worse for drink sitting on the bar amid signs of a struggle. I knew him quite well and he made no difficulty about accompanying me back to Wyton. He had challenged some locals after hearing derogatory remarks about the Royal Air Force and a brawl had resulted – broken glass strewed the saloon bar and he had the biggest 'shiner' I had seen to date. His opponents had departed and he was sitting there singing 'Ops in a Wimpy – Ops in a Wimpy – who'll come on Ops in a Wimpy with me?' to the tune of *Waltzing Matilda*. An admiring barmaid was tenderly sponging his black eye, or attempting to do so, and a furious manager wanted to know who would pay for the damage. In the middle of the discussion a large police officer arrived – a most sympathetic man who was persuaded to allow me to remove the officer, after hearing the account of what happened. Provocation? Who would stand by and hear his own service denigrated? Wasn't this the spirit of the war against the Nazis? 'Certainly, sir – I'd have done the same thing myself.' A most understanding individual. The damage was settled up and we heard no more. My young officer got a wigging next day – not a very severe one – and was lost a few nights later – cheerful to the last.

More than 700 bombers took part in the raid on Hamburg during the night of 24th July. I briefed the squadron late in the afternoon and the atmosphere in the briefing room was tense: it was a maximum effort and the Battle Order posted up on the wall beside the large map of Europe indicated the fact. I and both flight commanders headed a list of experienced crews with no 'freshmen' included; marking and backing-up duties were only to be undertaken by those who had done it before. Sixteen Lancasters with one in reserve stood out on the dispersals and the maintenance crews had been toiling from the moment the bell went for Hamburg. Weather promised fine for the night so that both bomber and night fighter were to be favoured in equal doses – and the Hamburg defences, both searchlight and flak, would be stretched to the limit dealing with such a heavy and prolonged assault.

Oboe couldn't help us – the range was too great – but the airborne H_2S could be employed to advantage since the contrasting areas of land and water would present a sharp image on the cathode ray tube in the navigator's compartment. The attack was to open with a drenching of high intensity flares – globes of brilliant magnesium hanging in the sky – and by this means eight selected Pathfinder crews would pick out the aiming point with the naked eye and mark it with red target indicators. No less than fifty experienced crews would 'back up' the reds over the full period of the attack and keep the pot boiling. Should cloud or smoke obscure the city then reliance would be placed wholly on the H_2S radar.

Such was the plan and the old hands heard it in silence – the mixture as before, they thought. They were wrong; and in the next few minutes the significance of the bundle of aluminium

strips in the hand of the signals officer was explained: this was
Window, another gift from the 'back-room boys' who laboured so
hard to make life easier for the perspiring crews over the enemy's
territory. We never met them – the boffins were a strange breed –
but we knew there were eminent scientists who did a great deal for
the war effort and though never seen at our level whilst we were
familiar with the products of their genius.

'Countermeasures' was the latest word in bomber terminology
and this bundle of metallised paper was the outcome of many
months of trial and error. Great quantities of this material arrived
on the station only a few hours earlier and, whilst we were at
briefing, the little bundles were being loaded into the bomb
aimer's compartment of each Lancaster.

There was a certain amount of amusement as the method was
explained – the history of dropping paper over Germany was not
a happy one. In the past we had off-loaded millions of sheets
prepared by the psychology cranks telling the enemy he ought to
give up, and a little later we had dropped German ration cards
designed to create confusion: neither had any visible effect as far
as we knew, and the task was hateful to most. Indeed, it was
rumoured the Germans were grateful since paper was in short
supply and the stuff we dropped was of a convenient size –
gathered eagerly by the townspeople to fulfil a special domestic
role. Hence the laughter, though it was noted the aluminised
strips were more fitted for the Christmas tree than the toilet on
this occasion. Patiently, the Signals Officer unfolded the plan for
spoofing the enemy radar: our approach would be masked by the
reflections generated by the strips and identification of individual
aircraft would be difficult if not impossible. This sounded good
and we went along with the idea, though the duty imposed on the
bomb aimers was irksome: each separate bundle to be dropped by
hand, after cutting the string, at minute intervals starting at a
given point some distance before the target. Take-off was set for
1025 pm.

Back in my room in the mess I had a presentiment about
Hamburg. This was to be a big effort and the enemy would know
all about it soon enough – casualties were going to be heavy.
Ground defences were better than average and there was a moon
for the ever growing number of night fighters. We never got away
with anything less than a pasting in this corner of the Reich and
what would even a moderate success add to march of events – a

few thousand killed and injured on both sides and a repeat performance the next night with a similar result? As for the strips of metallised paper – well, we'd seen a lot of war and every new gimmick had its counterpart. Whatever happened, I would have the usual letters to write next morning – to next of kin; endeavouring to convey a genuine grief to a stricken family – clichés – kind words and one sought hard for a change of phrase at times. Every boy was unique to his own family – and the letter one wrote would be kept for many years as evidence of courage and patriotism: it would be wept over and handled by many before becoming a treasured remnant of what used to be. Like all squadron commanders I endeavoured to pen a simple, friendly and sincere note of sympathy and because it was written by the man closest to the missing airman it counted. Thus, such letters were never stereotyped; they were personal and frequently took a long time to write.

As the darkness settled on that warm summer evening I completed my pre-flight checks in company with my crew and set off on a quick tour of the dispersals to make certain there were no last minute snags. When I approached the first aircraft of 'A' Flight I observed the captain standing by the rear door with his crew huddled around him – I knew what this was all about and had no wish to disturb them. They broke up and I had a word with the captain – a serious youngster and a man of considerable character. It was his habit to call his men together for a little blessing on the night's enterprise before entering the aircraft: few knew of this and those who did made no comment. It was strictly their own business and as a crew they lacked nothing in guts and initiative: he had them well in hand and they were inseparable.

For those who might smile at this somewhat unusual attitude, I can only say that this crew was highly respected and popular: we all varied in our choice of a talisman whether it be a St Christopher or a rabbit's foot but whatever the form it was one's own affair. This captain brought his Lancaster home after a savage encounter with a Ju88 on one occasion and made light of it – safe and sure in his particular beliefs. His handling of the Lancaster that night was masterly and at one point all electrical power failed leaving him without communication or dash lights to see his instruments – bomb doors trailing and undercarriage dropped, canopy wrecked and great holes in the fuselage but he was able to get as far as the long salvage runway for badly damaged aircraft at Woodbridge and the crew walked away from it! He was still flying when I handed over command of 83 later in the year and I believe he survived the war.

Weather was good all the way across the North Sea and into the Heligoland Bight where we altered course to a south-easterly heading and made for the estuary of the Elbe. They knew we were on the way from many sources of information, including the scattered fishing boats lying off the Frisians who reported by radio tho' this was late in the proceedings: the tall Wassermann radars looking east from the flat coast of Holland had picked us up before we reached the Norfolk beaches and this coupled with the usual signals activity which preceded the launching of a big force had the enemy fighters warming up their engines for the fray. Ross was busy in the nose off-loading his little bundles of metal covered paper strip as we entered the Bight and climbed a couple of thousand feet extra for the run in to Hamburg. I saw the enemy coast approaching and the searchlights sweeping the sky whilst ahead the heavy flak was engaging the first Pathfinders. The flares dropped in that same moment and the sky was filled with great blobs of white lights as we drew near the city: I had never before seen such a concentration and the outlines of Hamburg were plainly revealed. We were among the heavy stuff by now and observed the first group of red target indicator markers slightly to our right which did not satisfy Ross: he called for the bomb doors and concentrated on a further group believing the first reds to be an undershoot. He was right as our camera was to confirm the following day.

In a solid welter of heavy flak we continued across the city but to my astonishment we were unmolested by the scores of searchlight beams which flicked across us without taking hold, and nowhere did I see a fully formed cone working. This was most extraordinary but we were not disappointed with the quantity of flak bursts – they came thick and heavy on the bombing run – peculiar stuff which whizzed about the sky with a Catherine-wheel effect – very nasty and something quite new. Up it came then 'Bang' and it seemed that the sky was full of whizz-bangs – like the sparks flying off a whirling firework. A bomber blew up with a great sheet of flame as we went in for the drop and I felt the familiar rumble as our 1,000-pounders and target indicators left the bomb hooks. Then the little red light signalled from the dash that the camera was exposed so, willy-nilly, we stayed straight and level, wishing the seconds away so that we might be free of its dictate. All this time the searchlights continued to weave crazily – failing to lock-on and no fighters were seen.

After completing the photo run I pulled away to starboard and looked down on the city where large explosions heaved up with gouts of flame and vast fires were spreading. For once I had no doubt in my mind as to the accuracy of the marking and we observed the red glow of burning Hamburg from well out to sea. No night fighters followed us though we maintained a strict watch and corkscrewed steadily for many a long mile from the German coast.

The mystery of the crazy motions of the searchlights and the apparent absence of night fighters was soon explained: *Window* was responsible, creating utter confusion, and the fighter controllers on the ground were 'doing their nuts' to assess a situation which lacked any mark of sanity. The gun laying radars were all but useless – the little strips of metallised paper producing a blur on the cathode ray tubes and making a complete nonsense of everything: only the sheer weight of the flak barrage made any contribution to defence and our casualties were light indeed – twelve bombers only being lost. Full marks for the boffins who saved many lives that night over Hamburg and we owe them much. However, all was not over for me and my crew.

We arrived back over Wyton and I commenced the preliminary circuit of the airfield in poor visibility. Downwind of the main runway I flew in the area separating Wyton from its satellite airfield called Warboys – only three and a half miles distant. Both airfields operated a left hand circuit. As I passed the easterly end of the runway on my final circuit and commenced my landing checks I saw the runway lights fade in the murk and noted my distance from the airfield beacon which was barely visible. This provided a useful check in bad weather and I intended to keep it in view as long as possible.

Suddenly, in the gloom, I saw a great black shape rushing towards me and instantly stuffed the nose of the Lancaster down. He passed overhead striking my mid-upper turret and carrying away the starboard fin and rudder: only a fraction of a second saved us from a full collision and a certain exit from this world. The Lancaster yawed madly and, with only the port fin and rudder to assist me, heavy pressure was needed to keep the aircraft straight; the unbalanced controls left me with little or no manoeuvrability and I cursed the fate which had led me into this fix. I called the mid-upper gunner but he did not answer and I feared he had lost his life but George Coley was always the lucky one – he had been about to vacate his turret a few seconds before it was swept off the back of the Lancaster!

Gingerly I eased her round to a point where I began a careful approach on the runway threshold. Using the engines to control the turn and with the runway lights visible, I made ready to set her down after alerting flying control. Airspeed was critical and she behaved in the most awkward manner possible – swinging off centre and coming back again after a nudge on the throttles but we made good progress towards the runway. At the critical moment, when I was about fifty feet above the threshold, a Mosquito shot in front of me – a 139 Squadron aircraft – and landed straight ahead. There was no possible chance of going round again for another try at landing and I put her down on the grass at the side of the runway without incident.

This was more than enough for one night and I wiped the sweat from my brow. It was a minor occurrence though noted in the Official History; 'Of the missing aircraft five or six probably owed their destruction to night fighters and five or six to flak. Among those damaged two Lancasters sustained injuries in a collision over Wyton.' The aircraft which nearly ended our careers belonged to 156 Squadron: he got down on Warboys airfield with one engine on fire and the propeller missing from another. Squadron Leader Sammy Hall, a lifelong friend, was the captain and he admitted later to being a very frightened man. He was not alone. To cop it over Germany was bad enough but to exit as the result of a crazy mix-up in the airfield circuit following a successful run over Hamburg was the saddest thing ever.

The temptation to relax once in sight of home had to be resisted: crews were invariably tired after many hours in the air, with nerves screwed up to concert pitch for much of the time, and the sleep which followed was often interrupted, so that a sustained period of night attacks took its toll. I don't doubt that we lost crews through sheer fatigue occasionally – reaction to what the enemy was doing – one had to be quick with a fighter on one's tail. There was no second chance – no excuse accepted – it was all too late when the 20-mm cannon shells ripped into the fuselage: a dozy, half frozen gunner or a slack captain and it was curtains for the crew. Six hours for the Ruhr, eight for Berlin and ten for the far-flung targets was the routine. In winter the two gunners suffered miserably from frostbite, cramp and the motion of the aircraft – isolated from the rest of the crew theirs was a lonely vigil and I'm afraid we took them for granted most of the time. In 83 Squadron we possessed an outstanding gunnery leader in Johnny who set an example and brought to the functions of the air gunners a degree of importance which was thoroughly justified. He flew on every operation and exercised strict discipline on the ground: no squadron commander was better served in this regard.

The tribulations, trials and fears of a squadron commander were not confined to the business of bombing Germany. After the third successive attack on Hamburg, one of my aircraft returned with no brake pressure and I ordered the captain to land on the two-mile long runway at Wittering: he acknowledged and I thought no more about it: there was plenty of room for the Lancaster to run on without brakes after touch down. Having seen the rest of the squadron through interrogation, I went to bed only to be called almost immediately and informed that one of my aircraft was sitting in the middle of the River Nene. The crew were all safe and what did I want done about the stranded Lanc? 'Nothing', was my answer and I endeavoured to get to sleep. How, in heaven's name, had this aircraft got stuck in a river?

In the morning all was made clear: the crew had mistaken the runway lights of a potty little grass airfield occupied by Flying Training Command for those of Wittering. There was but six hundred yards of landing run available for Tiger Moths or something similar and the huge Lancaster had over run it – shot across the road – and down a steep bank into the river. The captain was not greatly experienced but knew enough to bring off a simple diversion in moderate visibility.

When I arrived at the little airfield near Oundle I couldn't believe my eyes: there was this great big aeroplane straddling the river with the water lapping the mainplanes. Had the undercarriage not collapsed she would have stood proud and the whole affair took on a comedy touch: she was little damaged and the locals had gathered in crowds to muse on this extraordinary scene. Nothing quite like this had happened in the memory of man. Salvage was impossible – she had to be broken up and Bennett, I remember, was not amused.

I believe fatigue had much to do with this incident – the crew had been to Hamburg three nights out of five, which was about average around this time and the last sortie had used up much of their staying power: they had not been given time to get into the swing. The crew, of course, was vastly more valuable than the Lancaster and this was the one bright spot: they did very well afterwards but, alas, were lost over Berlin the following January. The reason I remember them so well lies in the fact that it was this crew's final sortie which eclipsed George Ross, my own bomb aimer, who was a particular friend of the captain – Pilot Officer King – a very likeable young Australian officer.

In the light of the foregoing it is not remarkable that individuals should endeavour to make the most of a day freed from the pressures of war – the squadron simply melted into nothingness after a stand-down had been notified. One moment the crew room was bang full of young officers and NCOs and the next they grabbed their bicycles and it was too late for any recall. What did they do and where did they go? In high summer the river drew many whilst the more earnest went into Cambridge: as the evening approached one could be fairly certain of finding a number at the Pike and Eel or the Ferry Boat, down stream from St Ives, whilst the Green Man at Grantchester had its share of custom.

'Robbie' favoured the Red Lion at Whittlesford where we met some very friendly Americans from Duxford – fighter boys who flew alongside the Fortresses and Liberators of the Eighth Army Air Force. What characters they were – and how they made us welcome! On one occasion we were invited to their Officers' Club where a party was in progress and I remember Robbie's astonishment at finding the entrance hall chock-a-block with one armed bandits. Their colonel, a tall Texan, did everything to make us feel at home: the party was warming up and a bus load of girls arrived. There was no shortage of liquor and a band hammered out dance tunes. In a haze of smoke and bourbon we stood and watched the fun when a young lieutenant, dragging a dizzy blonde by the arm, accosted Robbie. 'Colonel's compliments, sir – this one is yours for the evening.' Robbie was startled – he wasn't one for women in that kind of setting – but he was courteous as usual and thanked the colonel for his hospitality, passing the girl on to another officer without the least embarrassment. We left around midnight and returned to Wyton as the alarm went for German raiders in the area.

The ante-room was empty save for George Coley, my mid-upper, who was wandering around with a full basket of eggs:

there'd been a little get-together and he was the only one left, a bit the worse for wear but fully in control.

'What on earth are you doing with those eggs, George?'

These items were in very short supply. He put a finger to his nose and a cunning look came over his face. 'I have discovered a secret source, sir. It's highly confidential. Would you care for a couple of eggs, sir?' He grabbed two eggs and endeavoured to press them into my hand.

'Very kind of you, George, but I can't use them at the moment.'

'Never refuse what the gods offer, sir – beautiful eggs – look at this one,' and he fished out another perfect specimen.

'You can't eat all those, George. What are you going to do with the rest?'

He looked at me in solemn fashion and spoke quite slowly. 'I will tell you, sir – confidentially – I – am – going – to – put – them – into – the – group – captain's – hat, sir. And he lurched off to the entrance hall where the brass bound hat reposed as usual on the small table.

'I don't think the group captain will eat all those, George, do you?'

'No, sir, he will certainly not eat them. Oh no, he will not do any such thing. Eggs are not for group captains sir. I intend to break them first.'

I persuaded him to go to bed.

In the morning I received two nice boiled eggs when I sat down to breakfast.

Bennett, who was always endeavouring to improve our mode of tackling the heavily defended targets, spoke to me in early August about the possibility of introducing tighter control of the bombing: greater concentration and fewer wasted bombs was his aim. There was nothing new in this although the term 'Master Bomber' was not yet in common use: the idea had been tried with varying degrees of success and Gibson's role in the attack on the Möhne Dam is a good example. Whether the same principle could be adopted in the case of a heavy attack by a large number of aircraft was not certain and he intended to experiment – suggesting that it might be tried out on one of the Italian targets in the first instance. At this time, Italy was the focus of attention and a series of raids were planned in an attempt to assist General Badoglio to make up his mind and throw in his lot with the Allies. There was much unrest in Northern Italy and the war was far from popular with the people who desired peace and an end to the German occupation. Badoglio was cautious and playing for time before he rolled his dice: a few sharp attacks by Bomber Command on the industrial north of Italy, where the population was densest, might well clarify his thinking and we stood by to strike across the Alps once more.

Turin was laid on for the night of 7th August and my squadron was called to produce only one Lancaster carrying myself and crew in the capacity of 'Master of Ceremonies' (that was the description of the task, and coined by Bennett). Whilst I thought it a trifle comic at the time, it didn't make much odds and I left Bennett's dinner table that evening and took off for Turin in pelting rain with but a vague notion as to what I was about to do. He had briefed me with his customary thoroughness, but there were several unanswered questions in my mind and it was a matter of 'playing it by ear' on the first time out. Later, I was to discover it was a rehearsal for something much more important.

I had enjoyed a good dinner and another American general was present, very similar in character to General Anderson whom I had met a bit earlier: these Americans favoured Bennett's organisation – they seemed to think we were closer to the sharp end than most and there was plenty of goodwill. This general drank a fair old tot from time to time and begged to be taken along but it wasn't possible. He was the only one imbibing, since Bennett didn't touch the stuff and I had a job waiting which allowed small leeway in that direction. He was a nice man, large of stature and sincere – a little voluble on the subject of bombing by his own airmen but none the worse for that. Bennett contrasted strangely with his chief guest but he was a good host, never obtruding his own aversion to alcohol and tobacco, but keeping the conversation flowing in easy fashion. I made my excuses, leaving the table for the flights and the general shook me warmly by the hand, breathing a gentle waft of whisky into my face as he whispered, 'God bless you, son. Come back safely.' He meant it.

Turin, like most Italian targets, proved a simple and easy operation: we sat over the city for the duration of the attack and the only real contribution we made was that of stemming the 'creep-back' – a phenomenon with which we were all too familiar and one which wasted much time effort and bombs. Once a target was under attack a tendency to undershoot set in with a cumulative effect as successive waves of the Main Force arrived, until a 'tail' extending back along the line of approach was clearly visible. Part of the reason lay in the difficulty of distinguishing the centre of the marking pattern and part in the readiness of some crews to release without taking the necessary care to establish the aiming point. This was the first occasion during which I had remained over a target throughout the full period of the raid and was able to judge the consequences.

Turin was no great shakes. The Italian gunners put up some rotten shooting and the searchlights remained inactive with their beams pointing upwards – abandoned most likely. The main value of the exercise lay in practising the use of the new VHF air-to-air communication and I continued a running commentary much to the amusement of my own crew. Air Commodore 'Bruin' Boyce, built like a small Teddy Bear and Bennett's Senior Air Staff Officer, was a passenger in the Lancaster. A few nights later I suggested to Boyce we might try it over Nuremburg but he refused to consider the idea. Thus I thought it was merely a 'one off' and we should hear no more of the 'Master of Ceremonies'. I was wrong and Boyce had his reasons for turning down the suggestion.

Three attacks were made on Milan between 12th and 15th of August and the wretched Italians were heavily pounded in the belief this would speed up surrender. This was an easy period after the Ruhr and 83 Squadron completed 175 sorties without a single casualty. This was just as well; the Battle of Berlin lay not far off and, in between, a novel excursion was exercising the minds of the planners. Bennett was driving hard – training, training and still more training – better equipment was forthcoming – tricell flare chutes enabling more light to be thrown on the objective – whilst training in the use of H_2S received impetus. Despite past failures, Bennett had great faith in this equipment: he believed it was a mathematical solution, a logical approach to the age old difficulty of seeing in the dark.

Alongside, our American allies grew in strength almost daily and their huge 'circuses' became a common spectacle over Huntingdon. We had little personal contact, save through the more senior officers who called on Bennett, and I was surprised by a request from their 306th Bomb Group to talk on the subject of night operations: it seemed they were considering a switch to night bombing following their heavy casualties in past weeks. I took a number of officers with me and each gave his own experiences to a packed nissen hut at Thurleigh near Bedford. The survivors of those desperate encounters were a group of serious and silent men; the wounds inflicted on the gallant Eighth Air Force had made these youngsters veterans almost overnight and they sat glumly facing the rostrum – one could have heard a pin drop.

I had no prepared brief and felt nervous: their colonel had asked me to talk about night tactics, enemy defences and our methods of dealing with searchlights. I felt there was little I could add; after Schweinfurt and similar battles they would know as much of war as I did myself: in fact our own casualties were light by comparison. Yet they were to batter on, continuing the big daylight formation policy whereas we, after the suicidal ventures into the Heligoland Bight in the first few months of the war, had abandoned it and sought the blanket of the dark.

They eyed me curiously but listened attentively whilst I ran through the activities of the opposition by night; then I handed over to Johnny, our gunnery leader. He was a good speaker and talked authoritively on a subject of profound interest – defence of the bomber – and there were many questions after he finished. Young, fresh-faced and drawn from many walks of life they had been thrust into a violent combat against professionals who gave no quarter: their future was questionable and they knew it. We had little in common save our casualties: the briefing room, like our own at Wyton on occasions, held an odour of death.

After each of my team had spoken, we held a further session during which many questions were put to us. An American sergeant got to his feet and, looking directly at me, asked what had been my worst experience and in my opinion the most dangerous. It was all deadly serious and I attempted to lighten the situation, pausing as if giving earnest attention to the matter before making a reply. They waited anticipating something terrible 'All right, I will tell you. It was in the New York Subway at the rush hour, where I was nearly trampled to death!' Roars of laughter and the spell was broken because the next man on his feet wanted to know how many women we had on the station. This was answered by one of my officers: 'Two hundred – mostly blondes.'

This was satisfactory, and for a while we circulated among the American crews talking to individuals with great friendliness on both sides. They were splendid chaps, wanting to talk about home and the families they had left behind and the war could wait. Few had established any kind of relationships locally and there were few diversions so that life on the base must have been pretty dull for them. The American equivalent of our own WAAF had not arrived and they were keen on meeting our girls.

Later, when I had command of RAF Warboys – a nearby airfield – a colonel telephoned me from Alconbury, another American base. This was at a time when we were experiencing sneak raids by the Luftwaffe dropping out of the low cloud and plastering anything resembling an aircraft. Orders had been received to dig small slit trenches around the perimeter which would provide instant cover for men working out on dispersed aircraft and something like eighty trenches were necessary. This was a first class chore absorbing many man-hours but it had to be done. The American who telephoned me had received similar instructions and the conversation was conducted on the following lines,

'Say, John. This is Colonel Smith. About these dam' slit trenches – how many have you got to dig?'

'Near enough a hundred, Colonel. What's the problem?'

'No problem. Now listen to this; I've got a machine that digs a trench in five minutes. In fact I've got two of these contraptions and you can borrow one, how's that?' This was generous to say the least.

'Very kind of you, colonel. Your offer is much appreciated; your machine will be a great help.'

'Sure it will that, John. Save you hours of sweat. Now, maybe we can do a deal – I need some help myself. What do you say?'

'Of course, glad to do anything we can. What's the problem?'

There was a pause whilst he chewed over his answer, then, 'Well, it's kind of tricky – but I guess you'd do a lot to get hold of one of my machines eh? Well, here it is: we're holding a party in the Officers' Club – a dance you might call it – and that's where I need the help.'

'Anything we can do, colonel. Is it a band you want.'

'No, no – we've got a band. It's women: you have a lot of those WAAF girls on your base. How about letting us have a hundred in exchange for one of my machines – just to make the party go, eh?'

The cunning fox, he'd led me within an ace of committing myself. I knew the 'Queen Bee' (senior WAAF officer) had very firm views on certain matters and watched over her girls like a mother hen. I said I would call him back then asked the Senior

WAAF officer for her reactions. I said nothing about the possible loan of the digger – it would have given the business a sordid aspect.

She refused as I knew she would – a hundred girls was out of the question but, on second thoughts she was prepared to let twenty go. 'And, of course, sir, I shall go along myself to look after them.'

And that was that. I believe they all had a good time. The colonel was disappointed but was sporting enough to send the machine over next day – arguing that I had short-changed him over the girls.

By the late summer of 1943 America was fielding a rapidly expanding bomber component in Europe and, considering the relatively short interval since they had entered the war, this was no mean achievement. As the months went by the full might of the United States became evident: committed to a global war with battle fronts in Europe, North Africa and the Far East their air strength was maintained at a high level of efficiency, sustained by a vast industrial capacity and a massive war chest. Though the build-up of the Eighth Air Force in this country was slower than first envisaged by the end of the year it was nearing a thousand first line aircraft whilst the provision of long range fighter escort was well under way. Following the disasters attending the Schweinfurt and Regensburg operation on 17 August 1943, they took the decision to escort the bombers, and in this way were able to pursue their declared aim of precision daylight attack, and we of the Royal Air Force Bomber Command were to see an unrealised dream fulfilled by our allies. There was little comfort in the thought that the swift escorting Mustangs were powered by our own superb Merlin engines and it was too late in the day to provide an RAF equivalent; we had to bat on through the darkness, groping for the target and wasting an appalling weight of bombs in the process. It is only fair to record that the Americans enjoyed an advantage in having handed to them the knowledge and expertise won so bloodily by the Royal Air Force during the first three years of the contest. This was an enormous contribution to their ultimate success and they were not unmindful of these benefits.

Anyway, we had the Lancaster – the world's greatest bomber of that day and drew comfort from that fact. The B.17 Flying Fortress was a fine aircraft, but it took no more than a third of the

Destruction in the V-2 rocket assembly factory in the Peenemünde Raid when John Searby was the Master Bomber.

The wrecked scientists' and other workers'

Lancaster's bomb load to Berlin since the dozen or so heavy machine guns and vast quantities of ammunition absorbed much of the pay-load. In American eyes this penalty was acceptable if it enabled a crew to fight its way through and bomb in daylight with a high degree of precision. Two tons of bombs dead on the pin are worth many tons scattered around the aiming point. Most of our attacks were of the 'area bombing' variety, but not all. The most accurate bombing of the whole war was done by the Royal Air Force and No 617 Squadron achieved absolute precision – dropping ten-ton monsters on the *Tirpitz* for instance – so that the Royal Air Force may fairly lay claim to both roles.

The crippling casualties sustained by the Americans in the late summer and autumn of 1943 brought into question the balance between aircraft lost and the damage done to the enemy. Quite apart from aircraft shot down, the degree of battle damage was severe and greatly affected the total numbers at readiness following a daylight raid on Germany. Enormous effort was put into repair after these attacks but the lesson was plain; no bomber formation was capable of defending itself against the ferocity of the German fighter attacks in daylight.

From the French coast onwards the battle was on: there was no diving for cover into the nearest cloud bank: formation had to be maintained regardless since each Fortress depended on the guns of the others for survival. The straggler was quickly cut to pieces and no quarter was given to a crippled bomber. We marvelled at the guts and heroism displayed by our American friends when these huge 'circuses' thrust their way into the heart of the German homeland: this was war in the air in the true sense but it could not continue for long; the strength of the gallant Eighth was being sapped in cruel fashion and, inevitably, a halt was called until escort fighters possessing the necessary endurance became available. The welding together of strong bomber and fighter groups into a composite striking force was of the greatest consequence.

United under one commander with a single aim, the threat to the enemy was formidable – the ultimate fulfilment of the Trenchard Doctrine. Unhappily for the Royal Air Force operating from these islands no comparable situation existed; we possessed no fighter element capable of performing a like duty.

During the Second World War, the Royal Air Force Bomber and Fighter Commands were worlds apart: we barely spoke the same language and in some curious manner a precedent, formed donkeys years previously in the British Army, had survived not only the move into the twentieth century but crept into the youngest arm of the Service – the traditional gulf between cavalry and foot soldiers. Guy Gibson, in his classic *Enemy Coast Ahead*, a book which carries the full flavour of war, devoted some space to the subject: 'Since the earliest days of the RAF there have always been two different breeds, different both by temperament and by virtue of their job, bombers and fighters'. He says much more and it is no part of this tale to delve into the details as Guy did: his experience of life in a fighter squadron and the general outlook makes amusing reading whilst his assessment of the task and characters of both bomber and fighter pilot is shrewd and apt. He was essentially a bomber captain and asked for a temporary transfer to a Fighter Command squadron to study night-fighter techniques. He might easily have stayed in fighters but chose to return to the heavy brigade, for reasons which are set out in his book. He refers to this period in his life as an interlude only, and was happy to find his way back to the 'Hams', whose airfields lay far from the cities and the fun and glamour of life on a fighter station. There is much horse sense in Guy's writings and I hope this famous biography never goes out of print, for it breathes the very spirit of loyalty, duty and devotion to all the things we most prize.

From mid-war onwards, Fighter Command, defending these shores, had never been under great stress; the enemy no longer posed any real threat to our cities and the accent had changed: all-out offensive action over Germany proper was the watchword which meant increasing the tempo and scope of Bomber Command. The escorting of the light bomber group in attacks across the Channel and a similar duty in respect of the American formations became the main occupation of the Spitfire wings until D-Day whilst a few night-fighter squadrons coped with the sporadic attacks by German nuisance raiders – and this was their lot. The strictly limited endurance of the Spitfire inhibited range, whilst the protection afforded to the outgoing bombers could not extend more than a few miles into enemy territory. The attempt to bring the German Air Force to battle was not successful since the enemy held all the cards and the main aim of the No 2 Group *Circus* operations was not accomplished. It was no fault of our fighter pilots – they lacked the right aircraft for the job, and many risked their lives in attempting to prolong their stay over the

Channel beyond the safe endurance of the Spitfire: the one item which could have brought new life and fresh laurels to the victors of the 1940 battles was absent – indeed it did not exist – and this was the long range escort fighter, designed for the task from the drawing board onwards. Had we possessed such aircraft in quantity the story of 1944 and 1945 might have been very different and Bomber Command's Rolls of Honour might well have been shorter.

Fighter Command was an entity, separate and distinct from other commands and its services had to be requested. The planning of bomber cover, over such ranges as the aircraft allowed, was conducted over the telephone and kept warm by bomber liaison officers. It was not enough. When Sir Arthur Harris ordered the first Thousand Raid he received little enough solid support from outside his own command. He records, 'Fighter Command supplied 29 aircraft to attack airfields along the route' and the response to his appeal for backing was finally whittled down to penny packets. Considering the vast spread of Fighter Command at that time, the contribution was petty when set against the launching of the strongest bomber force we could muster in that day. Sir Arthur was disappointed at the lack of enthusiasm, but at the same time it was made plain that he was on his own, and likely to remain so.

One may win a battle and yet lose the war: only by carrying the offensive to the enemy can it be won. The enormous increase in the strength of the German fighter force was evidence of the success of the plodding bombers and the drain on the enemy's resources, stemming from the need to defend himself, was an important factor in obtaining the final victory. Whereas at the beginning of the year, night fighter opposition was of small account, by August and September of 1943 it had become the chief obstacle in the path of the invading bombers and one expected at least one 'sighting', if not attack, on the way in and more on the way back from the target. This was but the beginning of the night-fighter scourge and in the following year it assumed such proportions that there were fears for crew morale. However we must now return to the events of late summer in 1943.

NOTES

1. John Searby was in the unique position of serving in front line squadrons in both of the groups – 5 (Main Force) and 8 (Pathfinder Force) – whose commanders were such rivals. The main sources of contention were about marking methods. Cochrane of 5 Group believed that the standard, high-level marking methods used by the Pathfinders could be improved upon, particularly by the use of low-level Master Bombers and marker aircraft carrying out the initial marking which could be backed up by further Pathfinders operating at the safer higher levels, and all bombing being carried out by the Main Force also flying at higher level. Bennett refused to attempt this method, saying that he would never commit any of his crews to dangerous low-level operations where the mass of German light flak could be so dangerous. Cochrane eventually proved that the tactic was possible, but only by using small aircraft at low level – Mosquitos and, later, borrowed American Mustangs – and only using small bomber forces in clear weather conditions. Bennett's Pathfinders, meanwhile, could mark any target, for any size of force, in any weather, though not usually with such accuracy as the 5 Group method when conditions were favourable for that method.

The effect of this rivalry was not much felt in the operational squadrons, except in the matter of reinforcement crews for the Pathfinder squadrons. Each Main Force group was nominally responsible for supplying a steady supply of partly experienced crews for particular Pathfinder squadrons. Thus, 5 Group was responsible for supplying crews for 83 and 97 Squadrons. But 5 Group was also responsible for keeping its own 617 Squadron up to strength and there were many criticisms that the best 5 Group crews volunteering for the special squadrons were being sent to 617 Squadron. Thus, Searby found himself in command of 83 Squadron and felt the effects of 5 Group's reluctance to send its best crews to the Pathfinders.

Later, in April 1944, Harris turned the whole situation upside down by returning 83 and 97 Squadrons to 5 Group and also giving 5 Group one of 8 Group's Mosquito squadrons – No 627 – so that Cochrane could operate 5 Group as an independent group with its own marking force. This move, which infuriated Bennett and many of the Pathfinders, is referred to by Searby in Chapter 9.

Coming back to Searby's comments on Embry and Bennett, he did not realize that Embry had actually been Harris's first choice to command the new Pathfinder Force when it was formed in August 1942. But Embry was 'not available' and Donald Bennett was selected for the appointment – a young, junior officer, thrust into the maelstrom of command politics and charged with creating a marking force out of the four ordinary squadrons transferred from the Main Force groups. It is fascinating to speculate upon how marking tactics would have progressed if Basil Embry had been the first Pathfinder commander.

CHAPTER EIGHT

Peenemünde

On the morning of 16th August I was called with my navigator and bomb aimer to Pathfinder Headquarters at Castle Hill House in Huntingdon. I had no idea as to what was in the wind but reporting to the Senior Air Staff Officer, Group Captain Boyce, we were led into a room where Donald Bennett stood examining a model – a large layout with buildings, bordering a section of coastline. The door was firmly closed behind us. Bennett welcomed us and came immediately to the point. This was a model of something we hoped to bomb in the course of the next day or two – very special and very secret. What we saw in that room was not to be communicated to anyone; we were to commit to memory what we saw on the table and he drew our attention to certain features. It was a factory of some kind – a development centre for special equipment – but the location was not disclosed.

He invited us to stay a while and take in any single feature which would enable us to mark the targets – three in number – extending in a rough north-to-south line. That was all – just make a mental picture for future reference because there must be no mistakes when the job came up – it had to be clobbered once and for all. Together we pored over the model; nothing is simple and by night the picture would be very different. George Ross, my bomb aimer, had an important role. Whereas Norman Scrivener and I would get the aircraft to wherever this special target lay in Germany much would depend on Ross peering directly down on whatever lay beneath. We might have learned more by relating the location to a wider landscape but we saw only the targets and a bit of what lay around. The coast was important – the buildings lay close to the sea and making the right approach would take us over the three aiming points, one after the other. At first sight it all looked fine. Nothing was said about the kind of attack planned for this objective – only that as a crew we might have to mark any single aiming point – and, whilst the operation was in progress, co-ordination between Pathfinders and Main Force would be my task.

I spent the afternoon on the river below Huntingdon, hiring my boat in the local village and pulling gently past Hemingford Abbots in the warm August sunshine. War – our kind of war – seemed a long way off: 36 hours earlier I had been over the Alps, attacking the Fiat Works in Milan. Now this.

In a bad week we might spend three or four nights over Germany and when the weather clamped down might well go several days without leaving the ground. Long intervals with no operations in prospect were bad for everyone – crews were bored since they had only the odd lecture to occupy them; PT was not viewed with any enthusiasm and local defence exercises only highlighted the defects in airfield security.

Viewed against the hardships of life at sea or the boredom of the army waiting for the day when they would assault the coast of Occupied Europe it wasn't all bad: there were compensations. When I left camp that afternoon the cricketers dressed in white flannels were going out to a smooth stretch of green set in front of the officers' mess, giving little thought to the war or what might be asked of them the following night. Yet the war was very close – the likelihood of a sudden exit lay just around the corner. You could knock up fifty runs before teatime and be wriggling your way through the flak and searchlights after supper! Life was full of surprises and each operation was different: the targets we had attacked on 10th and 14th of August provided a good example: Nuremberg boasted good solid defences and you had to watch it – both in terms of ground activity and fighter attack. Milan, at this stage of the war was a pushover, though the situation would change when the Germans took over the city.

The aim in attacking Milan was, as I have said earlier, one of helping Badoglio to make up his mind. Turin, Milan and Genoa lay within comfortable range of our Lancasters and each was a perfectly legitimate target; the first two cities possessed vast engineering complexes and the last was an important despatching point for German war material. Now, with the Allied armies driving the Germans before them out of Sicily and across the Straits of Messina, the Italians were in a bad way. The writing was on the wall: the 'red-hot rake of war' was about to be dragged up the long peninsula of Italy from south to north; the Fascist Government had fallen and we expected a surrender, though the Germans had other ideas and it didn't come.

This was a small raid using only 150 aircraft. In mid-France, and near Le Creusot, I saw one of our number shot down in flames: there was no flak burst, a night fighter was responsible. Normally, we did not encounter enemy fighters so far south, but it happened. He fell slowly, burning furiously, a single beacon in an otherwise peaceful setting, to explode in a tremendous gout of orange red flame – then nothing. Though I had seen it often before, this incident made me uneasy: we all took these Italian sorties with less caution than when flying over Germany. I learned afterwards this was the only bomber lost that night. A little later we were treated to the splendid spectacle of the Alps bathed in moonlight with Mont Blanc very prominent. As we swept over the last high ground before Milan I saw the two lakes, Como and Maggiore, on my left – stark landmarks pointing our path to the city.

In those conditions of bright moonlight we found and marked the Fiat Works for the force of bombers thundering on behind us, the red and green target indicators falling slowly to settle in a wide circle around the buildings. The heavy flak was badly aimed and inaccurate for height but the light flak streamed upwards endlessly, the tracer making weird patterns against the smoke of the fires, and the searchlights waving feebly in an attempt to engage a bomber. This was typical of the Italian defences.

It was a short attack and soon we were climbing back over the mountains skirting the Swiss border and passing close to Geneva – an island of street lights at the tip of the great lake; remote and sterile in a war-torn Europe. Sometimes the Swiss fired off their AA guns – though never with a hostile intent but merely to let us know they were there. Three hours later we landed back at Wyton after seven and a half hours in the air. This was Sunday, and we were stood down next day.

When I arrived in my offices on Tuesday morning – 17th August – I was informed that a *Goodwood* had been notified for that night. This was the code name used to inform all who needed to know that a maximum effort was required, but as yet the target had not come through. The squadron strength was normally sixteen Lancasters and we were going to be one short: nothing could be done about that since the aircraft was undergoing a major inspection and bits were scattered over the hangar floor. We had no reserve aircraft at the time and fifteen it would have to be. As for crews we were well placed: our losses had been light and on this day we had completed 175 sorties without loss – pretty well a record at this time. As for the target we were still waiting – they didn't lay on a *Goodwood* for nothing – could be Berlin by the fuel load ordered but the bomb load wasn't right – not enough incendiaries for the 'Big City'. At eleven thirty I was called to Group Headquarters where Bennett named the target as Peenemünde. The model we had seen previously would help us to identify the objective. With Norman Scrivener and George Ross I took another look at what we hoped to find.

Ten days had gone by since the Turin operation where we had tried out the 'Master of Ceremonies' idea and, in the interim, I had thought no more about it. Thus, I was mildly surprised when Bennett informed me he had decided to employ the technique on this occasion. I was to act as Master Bomber and stay over the target the full 45 minutes during which time 600 heavy bombers would pound the objective, allowing fifteen minutes for each of the three separate aiming points. The task of the Master Bomber crew was that of correcting the marking, if necessary, and directing the main force of bombers – concentrating them on the vital targets. Once again he stressed the importance of taking it out in one operation: defences were believed to be moderate only whilst identification ought to be easy since it all lay along the coast. Interception by night fighters constituted the main opposition: the planned route was similar to that we normally took to Berlin north about, over Denmark – and at briefing we learned that a diversion raid was planned over the 'Big City' to encourage the enemy in his belief that his capital city was about to receive another assault. It was to be a late take-off.

Squadron briefing took place during the afternoon. No indication of the nature of the target was given: I was instructed to warn my crews that failure to knock out Peenemünde at the first attempt would result in our being sent there the following night and the night after that until the place was flattened. This was the only gauge we had as to its importance. Nobody liked repeat performances; they brought heavy casualties. No 139 Mosquito Squadron, our neighbours at Wyton, would conduct a spoof raid on Berlin in an attempt to hold the German fighters a hundred miles to the south. The weather was favourable and we would have the 'benefit' of a full moon to light up the scene – a dubious advantage since it would not operate in our favour once the enemy fighters got among us. Nevertheless, it appeared this was a vital target and justified an attack in these conditions. As to the work of the Master Bomber, a piece of insurance was introduced by providing two deputies: if we were clobbered, then continuity was safeguarded. Wing Commander John Fauquier, commanding No 405 Squadron, would step in – and in the event of his meeting disaster Wing Commander John White of No 156 Squadron would be the next man up.

The briefing over I was introduced to a Government Minister, Mr Duncan Sandys, standing at the back of the room along with our own air vice-marshal, Don Bennett, and a number of people I had never seen before. It was not unusual to have visitors from the Air Ministry in London or Command Headquarters at High Wycombe, and sometimes politicians like Sandys, but they made little impact. They circulated among the crews in friendly fashion, asking questions, but they were surplus to the job in hand: they wished us well. One naïve gentleman asked my flight engineer if he thought there was a better chance of returning safely from Peenemünde than say, the Ruhr or Berlin. A stupid question answered by Frank with a smile, 'We'll just have to wait and see, won't we?'

Between briefing and take-off several hours elapsed: an uneasy period, and a common feature of life on a bomber squadron. The crews knew where they were going – had time to speculate on the outcome – but could not get on with the job until nightfall, killing time in various ways. It was mid-August, a long day of hot sunshine followed by a perfect evening with the sound of the reaping machine in the field bordering the dispersal area. The cold wet spring of that year delayed the harvest by a couple of weeks and I had watched the green corn turn slowly to ripeness and what promised to be a bumper crop. Now they were among it, the binding machine knocking off the succession of neat sheaves which marked its path round the field; the farmer in the driving seat of the tractor, his wife and daughter beginning the slow ritual of building the stocks, eight sheaves to each pile, set in tidy fashion, row by row. I knew them – though we had never spoken – and they usually waved to the Lancasters moving slowly along the perimeter track during the daytime.

At dusk I carried out the usual pre-flight checks, in company with Frank. The aircraft was loaded with high explosive bombs – 1,000-pounders – and yellow target indicators; the latter to be used to correct the marking if necessary. Our first try-out of the controlling technique at Turin didn't mean much; Italian targets were invariably poorly defended. The gun and searchlight crews didn't seem to have their heart in it and the searchlights often stood perpendicular – unmoving – silent witnesses to the character of the men who manned them. Not so with the Germans; I have seen the guns firing steadily amid a hail of 4,000-pound bombs dropped on Krupp's Works at Essen; Fritz never ran for shelter! On this occasion I had cause to ponder the business; past experience taught that specific aiming points were quickly enveloped in fire and smoke – and there were three separate targets. The first would present no problem but the second and third might well do so. A clear run over the objectives before the show commenced was essential; this would enable me to identify the three distinct features previously seen on the model. Five minutes would be sufficient providing all went well, after which I would pull off and await the arrival of the main force of heavy bombers.

At fifteen minutes to nine the silence of the dispersal area was shattered as our four Merlin engines came to life and we taxied out to the runway threshold. A quick brake check – flaps to take-off setting – line up facing the runway lights – the throttles were moved forward and Lancaster 'William' accelerated rapidly – tail coming up and the airspeed indicator needle moving round the dial to 100 knots when she left the ground sweetly to fly out into the twilight. At 1,000 feet we cruised comfortably over the familiar fenland scene with the towers of Ely Cathedral beneath my starboard wing tip; then on to Cromer on the Norfolk coast, the last sight of England for the next seven hours. The North Sea was calm and the sky clear above us as we made for the turning point where the bombers from the various groups spread between Yorkshire and Cambridgeshire would converge before turning due east to cross the Danish peninsula at the small island of Römö.

Timing is all-important and Norman, our navigator, makes certain we are dead on track. Constant vigilance is the first rule for survival: though we are flying at a low altitude it is by no means certain we can escape the powerful German radars situated on the mainland but we can at least make it difficult for the enemy. Both gunners scan the sky behind us and the radio operator stands in the astro hatch where he has a good all-round view whilst George covers the sky ahead. Head-on attacks have been a new factor in the summer months when the approaching bombers are silhouetted against the lighter western sky, and the superior speed of the enemy fighters makes this technique a distinct possibility.

I witnessed one of these lightning assaults, the enemy appearing as tiny specks ahead of us and slightly below: the closing speed was so rapid that they became little more than a blur, loosing off tracer shells at 600 yards range, flashing past us without scoring a hit. It was a one-off chance; the advantage lay in surprise and the fact that the only gun turret in the nose could challenge them, but hardly worthwhile in my opinion. I believe this strategem worked better in daylight and it was certainly employed against the big American Fortress formations later on.

'Enemy coast ahead'. This succinct phrase conveys an awareness that from now on we are over enemy territory – and it never fails to make an impact though we have heard it many times before. More than two hours have passed since leaving the Norfolk coast and George Ross, lying prone in the nose of the Lancaster is the first to see the shadowy outline of Römö and the mainland. Here and there we see small points of light, but the blackout in Denmark is rigidly enforced and these lights are burned deliberately – often as markers for the enemy fighters. The moon is now very bright and after flying at 200 feet over the sea for the past hour I pull up to 4,000 feet and pass swiftly over the enemy-held mainland. Light flak is the greatest danger to low flying aircraft; at 4,000 feet we are moderately safe.

By now the enemy is well and truly alerted: all over North Germany the night fighters are scrambling off their airfields. A big raid is on the way, but it appears to the fighter controllers that Berlin is the main target for the night. The 139 Squadron Mosquitos began crossing Denmark more than an hour ago and have convinced the enemy that the German capital is about to take another pasting. Thus, the defending fighters are ordered to Berlin though we are unaware of this as we pass over Danish territory on course for the island of Rügen lying north-west of our objective. In the moonlight I can see the whitewashed cottages on the southern tip of Langeland. The exhaust stubs of the Merlin engines glow redly and we feel pretty well naked: many eyes are now watching us – enemy eyes – and our Lancaster must stick out like a sore thumb since we are ahead of the main body by several minutes.

On the final leg to the target, small clumps of cloud appeared and later a sheet of stratus was encountered, but we flew beneath it and within 30 seconds of our planned arrival time saw at first hand the straggling complex we had travelling so far to find. Ross, my bomb aimer, Frank Forster, the flight engineer, and Norman Scrivener, our navigator, took a close look at it, as we flew close in bright moonlight. It was all there – the airfield at the tip of the promontory, the firing stands, the development and assembly halls and the large living site set out in the form of a horseshoe. Identifying the three aiming points, we circled the area as the light flak batteries opened up, noting smoke beginning to pour from hundreds of canisters set along the eastern boundary; thin trails at first but thickening rapidly and spreading across to the coast. I turned out to sea where in the light of the moon I observed two ships anchored. As we drew near they fired both light and heavy flak shells at us but the shooting was poor and we were in no great danger.

With two minutes to go before H-Hour, when the heavy bombing would commence, we waited for the preliminary marking of the first aiming point – standing off to north at a short distance from the coast. The method selected for the night was that of first illuminating the whole area with powerful flares and red target indicators dropped by the early Pathfinders using their H_2S radar equipment. By the aid of the white light thrown out by the magnesium flares the target would be marked visually by the most expert crews in the Pathfinder Force, using yellow target indicators which would burn for several minutes. This was a most exacting task and all depended upon the skill of these men, remembering time was short, allowing little scope for correction once they commenced their approach. Other Pathfinders, following on behind, would drop green markers on top of the yellows to keep the pot boiling. Thus, the main force of bombers could bomb either green or yellow unless ordered to do otherwise by the Master Bomber crew – and that was us – standing close by, maintaining a constant watch on the proceedings. Since there were three separate aiming points, the marking would be shifted every fifteen minutes until the task was accomplished. It was indeed a complicated operation, demanding the utmost in accuracy and timing and no rehearsal had been possible. My own aircraft carried a stock of these yellow markers which would be dropped to correct the marking if I deemed it to have gone astray.

Suddenly, the area was lit up by intense light from the falling flares amid which the single red markers – designed to assist the visual markers – shone vividly in dazzling cascade. George, our bomb aimer, gave an immediate shout over the inter-com to say the marking had overshot by more than a mile. He was most insistent but a moment later another clutch fell an equal distance to north to be followed by a single yellow marker plumb between the two. Immediately I broadcast to the approaching bombers ordering them to ignore all but the yellow, which was soon backed up by a mass of green target indicators. Wing Commander John White of 156 Squadron had dropped his yellows plumb on the mark and the credit for this effort belongs entirely to that officer. The high explosive dropped thick and fast covering the location of the Development and Research Works and we turned out to sea, where the flak ships had another go at us, passing round in a circle for another run over the aiming point.

Quickly, the area began to assume the familiar spectacle of a target under massive attack; bursting bombs, masses of billowing smoke, through which the sliding beams of the searchlights crossed and recrossed, the red flashes of the few heavy anti-aircraft guns – and yet we were virtually 'having it for free'. The defences were minimal and this happy situation continued for the full fifteen minutes allowed on the first aiming point. In this mish-mash of fire and smoke we could see very little and on our next orbit we flew lower when, to my horror the gunners informed me that they observed large 4,000-lb bombs falling past our aircraft. This was most alarming but was to be expected since so many bombers were flying well above the height at which we were orbiting. When considering how best to do our job, this possibility had not been taken into account – yet it was an obvious risk, and the likelihood of being walloped by a passing Blockbuster was more frightening than anything the enemy could do.

When the attack shifted to the second aiming point, marker bombs began falling to the south once again; overshooting by at least a mile. A broadcast to the main force and the oncoming backers-up largely corrected this error but a number of green target indicators began to drop into the sea and repeated warnings were given to stop this waste of bombs. Happily, this broadcast was heeded but the difficulties of the marker crews were increasing with every minute that passed. It was about this time that George Ross called me over the inter-com:

'Bomb Aimer to Captain – look out for fighters. A Lanc has just blown up over the target.'

I saw it almost in the same second. So, the real opposition had arrived and from then on the situation changed vastly. Silhouetted against the flame and smoke the bombers presented a clear mark for the attacking fighters and in the next twenty minutes we saw bomber after bomber set alight and crash into the holocaust below. The feigned attack on Berlin had been successful in containing the bulk of the enemy fighter force until the ruse was discovered and now they were streaming north, too late to save Peenemünde but determined to wreak vengeance whilst the opportunity remained. Nevertheless, the second aiming point was heavily plastered and we entered the third and final phase. Our task became increasingly difficult since the area below was confused – a veritable sea of flame and explosions – but on our fifth orbit a single group of Pathfinder markers was observed to fall smack on what we believed to be the right spot and I exhorted the last wave of bombers to ignore all else and go for them. Again we flew down the line of fires to turn out to sea with the flak ships sending up some very poor stuff.

The German fighters were arriving in strength. The full moon gave them every advantage; they stood on the wings of the conflict watching the approach of the relatively slow bombers then dived in with their victim showing up stark against the background of fire. Twin and single-engined fighters flew through the bomber stream careless of what was going on around them and the bright tracer shells were plainly seen, the bomber exploding and falling, a mass of burning fragments. Had we encountered the full force of fighters right at the onset of the attack it would have been a massacre; the respite gained for us by the efforts of 139 Mosquito Squadron over the 'Big City' swung the balance, causing numbers of the enemy to land and refuel before coming on to Peenemünde.

It was one o'clock in the morning; nothing more remained to be done. Those fifty minutes of time would remain long after other and similar experiences had been forgotten. We turned for home, finding comfort in the dark away from the fires. On our last pass across the target we turned to starboard instead of port saying farewell to the perspiring gunners on the flak ships. Lancaster William was now at the tail end of the stream of returning bombers; the show was over and if we could survive the attentions of the enemy fighters for the next couple of hours all would be well. Alas, our hopes were short lived for within a few minutes the battle was on again ...

'Rear Gunner to captain – fighter attacking from astern and

below,' and I heard the rattle of his four machine-guns in the same instant.

Heaving violently on the controls I brought the Lancaster round in a sharp turn, nose down – and the red tracers shot past without finding us. He was attacking in a climb and the nose down manoeuvre proved more effective than the turn. There was complete silence amongst the crew as we waited for his return and every man took a point of vantage from which he could observe the night sky. The Lancaster was diving, turning and climbing in a corkscrew motion and I expected the attack would come from the dark side, giving the enemy the best possible view of his target in the light of the full moon; a situation which allowed him to open fire at 600 yards if he so wished, well knowing our puny rifle-calibre machine-guns could not match his powerful 20- and 30-millimetre cannon.

The seconds ticked by and the sweat was running from the headband of my flying helmet when I heard Coley's voice from the mid-upper turret, 'Mid-upper to captain: fighter coming in. Starboard quarter down' and I made a sharp turn toward the attacker. Both turrets opened fire and I saw the enemy's tracer shells pass behind the tail. An excited shout from Flight Lieutenant Coley informed me that he had got in a burst, hitting the fighter, which disappeared. Since we did not see him crash, and this was no time to stay and look for him, we claimed him as damaged. Preece and Coley made a good team and I don't doubt we owed our escape to their efforts.

The fires of Peenemünde made an impressive glow as we sped on into the night, leaving Stralsund on our right as we crossed the Baltic coast to lose height over the sea. Any elation we may have felt over the apparent success of the operation was tempered by the knowledge that the German night fighters had taken a fearful toll of the returning bomber stream. Combats took place the whole way over the islands to the Danish mainland: conditions for interception were perfect. A Lancaster above and slightly ahead of us was hit I saw a small bright point of light grow rapidly until the aircraft was entirely visible – illuminated by its own burning fuselage. The fighter struck again and his tracers ploughed through the flaming mass which broke apart and plunged into the sea. A moment or two later another bomber exploded in mid-air.

Ahead of us the long bomber stream wound its way home. Small scattered cloud layers appeared but the weather was fine, the

moon casting our shadow on the surface of the water; our faithful
Rolls Merlins drummed on a fine even note. We were tired but we
had yet another two hours flying across the North Sea before we
would see the red flashing beacon which marked the home airfield
– Wyton. I touched down on the long east-west runway after seven
and a half hours in the air and the dawn was breaking after
making our report and returning to the mess for our hard-won
bacon and eggs.

The squadron suffered no casualties that night; the cost to the
Command was 40 heavy bombers and one Mosquito of 139
Squadron, mainly due to fighters. We never went there again and
the name Peenemünde disappeared from the list of targets; nor
did we know the true nature of the place. It was long after the war
ended that the name came into prominence and the significance
of this particular operation was understood. It has been stated that
the enemy's plans to saturate Southern England with flying bombs
and the dread V-2 rockets were set back by six months – a crucial
delay which pre-empted such a programme and bore heavily on
the success of the D-Day landings and subsequent Allied invasion
of Occupied Europe.[1]

The Peenemünde raid was soon followed by a series of raids on
Berlin. The first of these on 23rd August cost us twelve good
Pathfinder crews, including two from 83 Squadron – Flight
Lieutenant Brian Slade and young Reid; the former on his 59th
sortie and the latter on his 29th. Slade was an outstanding officer,
just 21 years of age; a short time earlier he had suffered engine
failure on take-off but pressed on to mark the target on his three
remaining engines.[2] Among the missing was Squadron Leader
John Forrest – a superb navigator – and among the first to
volunteer for Pathfinding duties.[3] Out of 710 dispatched 56 failed
to return on this occasion, including the twelve marker crews –
almost a quarter of the total casualties. This, the first of three
major attacks on the enemy's capital city gave cause for alarm since
a casualty rate of this magnitude could not be sustained. The
second and third in this short series resulted in 8 per cent and 6
per cent missing. The marked increase in the enemy night-fighter
strength was believed to be responsible for these comparatively
heavy losses and could well be taken as an indication of what lay
ahead in the pending Battle for Berlin. In fact, the bloodiest of all
the bomber struggles lay just around the corner – a battle which

e) Pathfinder Barons and
. From left to right:
o Captain John Searby,
Commander S. P.
ls, Group Captain
P. Collings, Group
in Hamish Mahaddie, Air
Marshal D. C. Bennett,
Tedder

') Searby and Flight
enant O'Brien at the
s Parade, 1st June 1951

Air Commodore John Searby, just before his retirement from the Royal Air Force

was to be both prolonged and bitter. Hamburg had been easy – Berlin was another matter.

The growing strength of the front line postulated the intake of large numbers of new crews quite apart from the need to replace casualties. Had there been no marker force, these inexperienced crews, dispatched independently to find and bomb targets far afield would, without doubt, have sustained severe casualties whilst the waste of bomb tonnage would have been massive. The existence of the Pathfinder Force enabled such crews to make an immediate and effective contribution, by simply following the experienced target markers whilst the force as a whole achieved a greater concentration which provided a degree of protection. Sticking closely with the crowd cut down the losses.

After the Munich attack of 6th September I was laid up for four days with, appropriately enough, German Measles which caused a certain amount of amusement. On the Munich raid the enemy laid long lines of flares indicating our approach path; these were very pretty to see, though I doubt that they got much profit from the exercise. Certainly, there were plenty of fighters but we got in and out again without incident. On the way home we flew a leg of three and a half hours back to the Channel coast, getting off track to the north of Paris and encountering a vicious attack from a single flak battery which had taken our height and speed with unusual accuracy, the stuff bursting within a hundred feet of our starboard wing tip. I was tired – the long haul back from the target had been slow, with a quartering headwind pulling the groundspeed back, and monotonous, so that the arrival of six bursting shells caused a sensation. By the time the second volley arrived we had lost height and made a sharp alteration of course but the lesson was plain – no more dozing at the controls. Often the bomb aimer would observe the muzzle flashes and warn me so there was sufficient time to take avoiding action, but on this occasion low cloud hid the guns.

A welcome visitor to Wyton was Bill Hughes-Jones, one time education officer and a friend of long standing going back to Halton where I first made his acquaintance. Now, dressed as a squadron leader on Intelligence duties he had lost none of his enthusiasm for people, places and his Welsh birthright. He was a most engaging man with the quality of making one feel that every problem might be surmounted, every difficulty overcome, provided one kept the aim in view. A scholar and an Oxford graduate he devoted years to writing books on ancient civilisations and the Prophets of the Old Testament; he was unworldly to an astonishing degree and his proudest achievement was his Mention in Despatches during the First World War when he fought as a young lieutenant on the Western Front.

On a stand-down day we went to Cambridge and walked in the gardens of Trinity College, then had tea in a little cafe in Petty Cury where he did all the talking and had me rocking with laughter at his exploits. In the days before the war, as the station education officer, he never had any money – every penny went on furthering the prospects of his son and daughter and putting them through the university – and rode an old bicycle to and fro from his digs in the nearby village. I was sometimes called on to assist with the teaching of the NCOs' class in such subjects as maths and map reading because Bill hadn't a clue; thus, when the results were published and fourteen out of sixteen candidates passed the written examination for promotion to sergeant he was over the moon, receiving a special letter of thanks from the station commander for his work. I recall his rushing into the Navigation Office in the hangar waving this piece of paper at me, the happiest man for miles around.

A visit to the Priestleys at Offord d'Arcy was time well spent. Arthur Priestley was host to many Pathfinders from the nearby airfields and in those delightful summer evenings one would usually find at least a dozen officers spread around his house and garden. They were a happy family with political connections and well abreast of events. I remember my astonishment on first entering the house to discover it jam-packed with people talking and laughing around a superb silk banner which bore the words 'Nice – Bataille des Fleurs – 1912' and Arthur's dissertation on the delights of that famous resort. Like my friend Bill Hughes-Jones he was a scholarly man – knew everybody and had travelled to most places. He was an elegant conversationalist – fascinating to people such as myself – and properly belonged, I thought, to a world which vanished in 1939, never to be seen again. A great letter-writer, his large hall stand was stacked with the correspondence of weeks and months – all in neat piles representing a unique filing system which he assured me worked very well. Arthur, his wife and daughters did much to relieve the stress of war and I remember them with the greatest affection.

The blocking of the Mont Cenis tunnel on the Italian border created a welcome diversion from the run-of-the-mill attacks on the heavily defended German targets. In bright moonlight we flew across France to Grenoble searching for the small town of Modane and the marshalling yards situated at the mouth of the tunnel through the Alps. Our target lay deep in a valley through which the enemy dispatched supplies to his troops in Italy. There was little in the way of ground defences and the attack opened with showers of red and green markers followed by high explosive, creating an awe inspiring spectacle: the bomb and photo flashes were reflected from peak to peak; it was indeed hell let loose whilst it lasted. Thousands of tons of rock and debris rolled down the mountain side – disturbed by the reverberations from the crashing bombs and the marshalling yards were useless for many a month.[4] This took place on 16th September.

NOTES

1. John Searby's successful flight as Master Bomber on the Peenemünde Raid was his most important operational flight of the war. He was awarded an immediate DSO for that night's work. I wrote a book about this raid in 1982; John helped with a personal contribution. He also wrote a book about the operation. I am reluctant to add too much to what he has written here but would like to make two comments.

  First, most of the initial marking and bombing fell on a wooden camp for forced foreign workers – mainly Poles – two miles south of the true target; about 500 of these workers were killed within a few minutes. John Searby detected this and warned the Pathfinders and Main Force crews to move the attack back to the main target. This was probably Searby's most important contribution to the raid. Wing Commander John White's yellow target indicators, as Searby recounts, swiftly remarked the main target. (John White and all his crew died over Berlin on the night of 18/19th November 1943.)

  Second, it was a common misconception that this raid affected the German V-1 flying bomb campaign. There was some test flying of V-1s from the Peenemünde airfield but the airfield was not included in the bombers' targets that night. The raid was directed entirely at the development and production of the V-2 rocket and, as Searby states, successfully delayed the introduction of a weapon to which Britain had no defence.

2. There is some confusion over Slade's age. Searby says 'twenty-one', the Berlin War Cemetery register says 'nineteen'; another source says 'twenty-two'. He was certainly a fine pilot; only his tail gunner survived when the Lancaster was hit and blew up on the approaches to Berlin. The seven-man crew had a total of 330 completed operations between them

before the night on which they were shot down.

Pilot Officer J.A. Reid and all his crew died when shot down very close to Slade's aircraft, both being on their marking runs into the target.

3. Squadron Leader Joseph Neville Forrest, DSO, DFC, aged 36, was in the crew of Pilot Officer Kenneth Fairlie, a young Australian pilot; all were killed, also shot down in the Berlin area. The bodies of Forrest and Fairlie were never found and their names are on the Runnymede Memorial.

4. This attack on the railway installations at Modane, on the night of 16/17th September 1943, was a failure, but a second attack on 10/11th November caused serious damage.

CHAPTER NINE

The Battle of Berlin

As the autumn of '43 drew on the pressures were mounting:
Stuttgart, Kassel, Hannover, Mannheim and Munich came under
heavy attack with complete devastation attending the fire-storm
raids on Hannover and Kassel. I was sad at learning of the death
over Kassel of Wing Commander Penman, who assumed
command of No 61 Squadron during the time I was at Syerston.
This was my last operation with 83 and memorable for our being
intercepted by a night fighter at the Belgian frontier, where I
corkscrewed to such effect that he gave up trying and we lost him
eventually. I think that I was as much influenced by the knowledge
that I was on the verge of handing over command of my squadron
as anything else since I was determined he should not have us on
this, my final sortie. Only 24 hours earlier a phone call from
Hamish Mahaddie advised me that 'the sands were running out',
to use his own words, and my replacement would be John Hilton –
a former flight commander in 83. The flak was brisk over Kassel
that night, one of our number sustaining a direct hit as he ran in to
drop his target indicators. Ahead of me the sky was full of burning
fragments which caused the German gunners to redouble their
efforts and they put up a long box barrage worthy of the Ruhr at
its worst.

On 5th November I handed over to Hilton, and he, alas, was
killed two weeks later over Berlin. A fine officer, and one of the
very first to volunteer for Pathfinder duty, he had been with
Bennett from the beginning: I could not have wished for a better
successor. Since there was no suitable replacement immediately
available Bennett asked me to return pending the arrival of a
relief, and Jack Abercromby eventually came from 5 Group in
early December. It was unusual to appoint an officer from outside
the Pathfinder Group but not unreasonable since 83 depended
upon 5 Group, in theory anyway, to supply replacements, and
Abercromby bore a good reputation. I was all for it because he
could be relied upon to see that his old group sent us other than

'pressed men'. Well, it didn't work out: he, too, was among the missing from the big attack on the 'Big City' not many days later – 1st January 1944 to be precise. He strongly favoured the straight and level flight path from base to target – spurning the use of evasive tactics such as the 'corkscrew' – and it was a case of putting in 'George' (the automatic pilot) all the way. This is no criticism of a courageous officer; he had his own methods and beliefs and in the hugger-mugger of a mass attack almost anything can happen – and often did so. I held the opposite view and in the short time we had together we discussed tactics, but he was adamant on the matter of evasion.

Looking back, the squadron record in respect of its commanders is depressing: Gilman, my predecessor was less than a month in command whilst Hilton and Abercromby disappeared within days of taking over. My friend Hamish used a phrase, 'the swing of the pendulum' and it may well be he was right.

Thirty-five attacks, comprising some 20,000 sorties, were flown during the overall Berlin campaign which began in November and terminated with the Nuremberg disaster of 30th March 1944: of these sixteen attacks totalling 9,000 sorties were directed against the German capital. Any gaps in the onslaught, stemming from weather and crew exhaustion, were filled in by the swift Mosquitos of Bennett's Light Night Striking Force. The vile weather, which was a feature of those winter months, and the necessity for creating diversions which caused the enemy to spread his defences, brought other major cities under the bombers. Nineteen attacks, involving 11,000 sorties, were made on widely separated targets in support of the main aim; delivered by between 700 and 800 Lancasters and Halifaxes on each occasion. Berlin was seldom clear of cloud, the city screened from view by low stratus with a few occasional breaks here and there. The task of the forecasters of Bomber Command Headquarters was indeed a difficult one and no opportunity was lost by the Mosquitos of the Meteorological Flight to ascertain conditions in advance of the attack, flying great distances over enemy territory at high risk. The information they brought back contributed massively to the success of the heavy bombers and the Mosquito crews were deserving of the highest praise. Unarmed and relying solely on their high speed they braved both flak and fighter interception times without number.

Throughout the winter of '43/'44, conditions on the many

airfields of Yorkshire, Lincolnshire and Cambridgeshire were severe: runways had to be cleared of snow whilst sheets of ice made for a tricky take-off with a 10,000-lb bomb load. The servicing of aircraft, the hauling of bomb loads up the slippery ramps from the bomb dump, the bogging of aircraft with a wheel off the perimeter track (by no means an uncommon occurrence) all added to the trials and tribulations of the patient ground staffs, but it was in the air that the more serious problems arose. In the words of Sir Arthur Harris:

> The whole battle was fought in appalling weather and in conditions resembling those of no other campaign in the history of warfare. Scarcely a single crew caught a glimpse of the objective they were attacking, and for long periods we were wholly ignorant, except for such admissions as the enemy made from time to time, of how the battle was going. Thousands upon thousands of tons of bombs were aimed at the Pathfinders' skymarkers and fell through unbroken cloud which concealed everything below except the confused glow of fires.*

So much for the target area; but first, the heavily laden bombers had to get there! The North Sea is notorious for bad weather in winter; ice is frequently encountered in the thick cloud layers and the big bombers, carrying a 3,000-lb overload were vulnerable to wing icing which destroyed the contour of the leading edges and reduced lift, in addition to increasing the all-up weight. In these conditions the bombers became unstable and whereas the Lancasters, possessing superior flying qualities, managed to survive, the Halifaxes suffered badly; the merest whiff from another bomber's slipstream could spell disaster in the worst case and a loss of several thousand feet of height in less critical circumstances. I observed a Halifax turn over, nose down, and out of control on one occasion – and that was in summer – the direct consequence of encountering someone else's slipstream. Even the Lancaster, above 18,000 feet, carrying the cursed overload imposed by Bomber Command Headquarters, wallowed, and became an easy prey for the attacking night fighter: the slick manoeuvre essential to evading the assault became impossible. It might·have been better to rip out the turrets; the guns were

---

* *Bomber Offensive*, Collins, 1947.

virtually useless, and the result would have been another fifty miles an hour increase in speed once rid of the weight and drag of the encumbering mid-upper and tail turrets. I was not alone in this belief; others held similar views.

In the Battle of Berlin, Bomber Command 'turned over' its full strength: in simple terms it replaced itself. The consequences were serious in that the experience of the crews was watered down and few squadrons could boast the 'screening' of crews who survived their full tour of operations, yet there was no evidence of any reluctance on the part of the raw crews fresh from training to step into the breach. In the Pathfinder Force the loss of squadron and flight commanders caused Bennett much grief: 7 Squadron suffered badly, losing such men as Ken Rampling, Fraser Barron and the incredible Lockhart. All were seasoned commanders, known for their courage and high qualities of leadership; the youthful Fraser Barron had come up from a mere aircraft captain to assume command of his squadron: a stout New Zealander his loss rang a tocsin throughout the marker force; he epitomised the 'press-on' spirit of Bennett's officers.[1]

The battle was unequal: the Ju88s and Me110s could down a bomber with the same ease that our Spitfires demolished the slow Heinkels during the Battle of Britain and the German pilots were imbued with a similar spirit; the defence of their capital city demanded the utmost in skill and determination and their growing mastery of the night skies induced a degree of confidence leading to their penetrating the bomber stream, regardless of collision risk, in pursuit of a victim. Over the target, the 'Big City', we saw the 'free lances' – single-seat fighters – scorning the flak bursts, intent at shooting down a bomber at all costs, displaying an arrogance and wilful disregard of their own ground batteries which spewed up the shell bursts. On the return journey of the bombers, the German fighters grouped around the holding radio beacons waiting for the final word before they launched themselves at the departing armada of Lancasters and Halifaxes.

The Battle of Berlin was not a defeat in absolute terms – but it was a battle we could not win. Sir Arthur Harris made frequent pleas for help from our fighter brothers, to send in their Mosquitos, but the resulting penny-packets made little impression. We needed hundreds of protecting fighters at this stage – not merely the ten or fifteen *Serrate*-equipped fighters led by the gallant Wing Commander Bob Braham. It was maddening to the bomber crews that the Rolls-Royce engined Mustang which escorted the American daylight formations up to the limit of their penetrations was not available to Bomber Command. The 'blanket of the dark' no longer sufficed to protect us: German search and lock-on radars had improved enormously by the end of '43, whilst the aircraft which carried them had doubled in strength. The heavy bomber

> belching flames from their exhausts as well as transmissions from their navigational and fighter warning apparatus, made them all too apparent to those who hunted them ... Once engaged in combat they had little chance of victory and not much of escape, while the large quantities of petrol, incendiary bombs, high explosive and oxygen gave spectacular evidence of their destruction.*

The long drawn out struggle for the enemy's capital, with its fearful toll of young lives produced many individual acts of heroism which went unremarked and which breathe the very spirit of Bomber Command. This was the high point of the bomber offensive and Harris's last throw to achieve the victory he believed could come from a succession of massive onslaughts designed to break the enemy's will to continue the war. Resolute in his aim, his frustration over the failure to secure a concentration of bombing on the selected aiming points caused him to seek alternate methods of marking these vital areas.

Bennett's Pathfinder crews – employing the most experienced in the role of visual markers – were often baffled by the prevailing low cloud which screened the city and recourse to purely radar marking using the airborne H_2S was only approximate owing to the confused picture on the cathode ray tube stemming from the reflective qualities of the built-up areas. The best radar operators – specially trained for these Berlin attacks – had great difficulty in defining a single aiming point amid the clutter on the screen. Time and again the assault went in without a single picture of ground detail being recorded on the camera in the belly of the bomber: and the crews reported scattered bombing when, occasionally, a brief view of what lay below was accorded them. The battle was nearing its end when Air Vice-Marshal Cochrane

* *Extract from The Strategic Air Offensive against Germany*, op cit, Vol II, p. 201.

expressed the opinion that Berlin could be marked successfully – and precisely – using a technique in which he had great faith. This was the low-flying Mosquito.

Sir Arthur had great confidence in Cochrane. Nevertheless, he spoke to his Pathfinder commander, Bennett, and told him all that Cochrane had said on the matter. Bennett was not convinced and pointed out the difficulties, namely, that of finding an exact point when flying a high speed at low level *by night* and in the face of both flak and searchlight opposition: in addition there was still the matter of the low cloud layer which would hide the target indicator dropped by the Mosquito. These objections did not please Sir Arthur; in effect Bennett was refusing to do it. The same day he sent for Bennett who flew down to High Wycombe to face an irate C-in-C – to be told he was to lose three squadrons to Cochrane – two heavy and one Mosquito – which would operate under Cochrane's orders and do the job.[2] This was a sad day for Bomber Command. The rivalry, if that is the right word, between Cochrane and Bennett was well known and not a few deemed Sir Arthur's action abrupt and indeed unfair. It all depended on how one viewed Bennett whose rise to fame had been swift and whom some considered both conceited and intolerant. No matter, the fact was that Bennett had borne the heat and burden of the day from the moment the Pathfinder Force was created – and had literally plucked success from a ground-bed of mediocre attempts to get the bombs on the target. Again, he was better qualified to pronounce on the problems of target marking by virtue ·of his experience and technical know-how.

Bennett's own book, *Pathfinder*,* reveals the bitterness he experienced over the loss of his squadrons:

> This was, in itself, a tremendous slap in the face to a force which had turned Harris's Bomber Command from a wasteful and ineffective force into a mighty and successful one. It meant in the eyes of the rest of the Command that, in the opinion of the Commander-in-Chief, the Pathfinders had apparently failed.

Few would agree with that last sentence: in no wise had Bennett's squadrons failed: in gallantry and loyalty to their C-in-C the Path-finder crews had wrought mightily. The destruction of Krupps,

---

* Published by Frederick Muller, 1958.

the devastation of Hamburg and the continual slogging away at every heavily defended target in the Reich tell their own story, whilst Bennett's constant endeavour to improve his marking methods and skilful employment of his Mosquitos in a diversionary role were well illustrated in a hundred encounters. Bennett lost his squadrons as a direct result of his blunt dismissal, however sound his reasons, of a scheme which Harris believed, had some merit and which, with a little more time to think about it, would never have countenanced.

Sir Arthur had immense faith in Bennett's powers: 'He was, and still is the most efficient airman I have ever met; his courage, both moral and physical, is outstanding, and as a technician he is unrivalled.' Again, in an oblique reference to Cochrane's group, 'I continued to entrust the Pathfinder Force with the identification of the target in nearly all our principal attacks until the end of the war.' Indeed he did so; all major assaults remained Bennett's responsibility.

Both Cochrane and Bennett had seen service under Sir Arthur; the former as a flight commander in the mid-twenties at the time Great Britain held the mandate over what was then part of Mesopotamia and the latter when Harris commanded a flying boat squadron. Thus, their qualities were well known to him. Whilst he admired Bennett's competence and sheer ability, he appeared always to incline to the aristocratic Cochrane. The Honourable Ralph Cochrane was both clever and able: his success over the Dams Raid undoubtedly strengthened a relationship born of long association and an undisputed claim to a place in the 'establishment' of senior RAF officers with roots going back to the birth of the service in 1918. He looked for the unusual – willing to chance his arm – ready to try something new and, with Harris's backing, he was often successful. He dealt with matters of administration coolly and deliberately – was never seen to display emotion and was quick to play down exaggeration or conceit. Sparing of praise he conveyed the impression that to give of one's utmost was no more than one's plain duty. Some thought him a cold fish; few doubted his ability.

Whilst Bennett was furious over the transfer he complied with Harris's edict and the three squadrons moved to No 5 Group never to return. I attended the 83 Squadron farewell party which was not the happiest occasion and where some gloomy prophet predicted the eclipse of the Pathfinder Force. The fact that

Bennett was expected to train and supply replacement crews to his lost squadrons rubbed salt into the wound! For the future he was required to continue marking targets as formerly and with the increasing demands made upon him after D-Day, when a variety of targets were attacked in a single day, necessitating an increased effort, the loss of two heavy squadrons more than doubled his problems over providing experienced marker crews. Such were the consequences of a brush with Sir Arthur Harris.

The success of the Dams Raid was to have far reaching results since it demonstrated a capability for making precision attacks upon selected targets by relatively small numbers of bombers, and No 5 Group was to excel in tackling a whole range of such targets. Nevertheless, the technique demanded special conditions embracing training, weapons and most importantly – weather. Whereas Bennett's Pathfinders tackled every heavily defended target in Germany, flying in all weathers as they did during the Berlin campaign, the specialised nature of the 5 Group attacks did not lend itself to the run-of-the-mill assaults performed by the bulk of Bomber Command, though Cochrane's squadrons joined in to swell the numbers. At the time of the formation of the Pathfinder Force, Sir Arthur Harris had been reluctant to accept what was primarily an Air Ministry proposition stemming from the Director of Bomber Operations and backed by the Chief of the Air Staff. He, Sir Arthur, favoured the forming of marker squadrons in each of the bomber group, eschewing the creation of what he called an élite force and it was only after a great deal of pressure had been exerted by the Air Staff that he gave way. Thus, when Sir Ralph Cochrane pulled off what Winston Churchill termed one of the greatest feats of arms (the Dams Raid) Sir Arthur Harris expressed his intention of reserving No 617 Squadron for similar exploits in the future. Though I don't think he ever said as much it is possible that he saw his earlier stand against a central marking echelon vindicated. Cochrane had put into Sir Arthur's hand a rapier which given favourable conditions could pierce the enemy with great precision as opposed to a bludgeon which crushed his industry and flattened his cities. But, Harris needed both weapons and one must complement the other: 'If the Americans will come in on it with us we can wreck Berlin from end to end.' The rapier had no role in the hugger-mugger of the Berlin campaign!

Despite the loss of 83 and 97 Squadrons to Cochrane, Bennett's

Pathfinder group still represented a significant slice of the Command as a whole: nine stations and seventeen squadrons which included the Light Night Striking Force of Mosquitos kept him busy. His handling of the Mosquitos, both in the diversionary role and the constant hammering of Berlin, was masterly whilst he retained full responsibility for the operation of the *Oboe* marking techniques and for the control of No 1409 (Met) Flight: the former reflecting his knowledge and grasp of this most precise and intricate mode of marking a target and the latter demanding a constant fund of long range weather information without which Bomber Command could not operate – and, indeed, other formations outside Bomber Command – covering 24 hours of the day. These aircraft were unarmed and flew ... 'deep into the heart of enemy territory, often in broad daylight, without any cloud cover'. The crews commanded our admiration and 'there were some harrowing experiences when they were intercepted, particularly by German jets, just toward the end of the war, which could outpace but not outmanoeuvre them. Their anxiety to run for home had to be overcome whenever the enemy closed, so as to take advantage of the Mosquito's ability to out-turn the enemy.'

The airborne radar H_2S, in which Bennett had great confidence and which he saw as the ultimate solution to the accurate marking of targets lying far afield, improved greatly with the introduction of the 3-centimetre version. This was a triumph for the backroom boys, the scientists who laboured at the Telecommunications Research Establishment, since the picture presented on the cathode ray tube was of finer grain enabling the operator to observe ground detail more perfectly. Long hours of training were devoted to this instrument and all crews joining the Pathfinder Force passed through the Navigation Training Unit at Warboys before joining the squadrons. After leaving 83 Squadron I was given temporary command of this unit to which Bennett was a frequent visitor and who addressed all new crews commencing the six weeks induction course. His grip of the technical aspects of the navigator's task and his enthusiasm made a profound impression whilst some remarked on the professionalism of a senior officer – an air vice-marshal – who quite obviously knew what he was talking about. A complete course of young Australian officers – mildly cynical and faintly rebellious, having burned all the furniture in the mess ante-room the previous night as a protest of the lack of adequate heating, fell into line without a murmur.

They were a cheerful crowd and the punishment I doled out (30 minutes' rifle drill each morning before starting work) produced a cheer when I turned up to see what was going on! There was no resentment; they had their fun and bore the consequences without protest. Lack of coal was a problem in the winter of 43/44, particularly out on the dispersed sites where the only form of heating was the ubiquitous iron stove – the famous 'Chattan Queen' with origins in the Crimean War.

The Pathfinder Force was achieving a certain vogue and not all who sought to join were of tender years: a few wing commanders, anxious to round off their careers with an operational command, went through the training course and did well later. Wing Commander Tatnall, who taught me to fly some nine years earlier and who relinquished the rank of group captain to join, appeared one day to my great pleasure. He must have been verging on 40 years of age but assimilated easily the role of a bomber captain, bringing considerable experience and a nice light touch which went down well with all who met him. After finishing his course he was posted supernumerary to No 7 PFF Squadron at Oakington with the likelihood of taking command eventually. Alas, he was missing over Berlin within a very few weeks. One of the old school he believed he had a duty to fight: his words to me on arriving in my office were typical: 'Well, I've had it cushy for a good many years and it's time I showed my gratitude!'[3]

With the move of the Mosquito Conversion Unit to Warboys came Wing Commander Roy Ralston, a friend of long standing whose record in the light bomber group starting with the Blenheim operations was second to none. As commanding officer he was responsible for training replacements for Bennett's Light Night Striking Force and *Oboe* squadrons. A quiet personality, Roy possessed a strong character and led by example; he was utterly fearless, demonstrating patience and determination – a quality which was to stand him in good stead when, in later years, he suffered ill health and was confined to a wheel chair. I never knew a man to bear the slings and arrows of outrageous fortune with more fortitude than Roy. He had achieved great things in his flying days and was struck down almost overnight, whereas he would without doubt have risen high in the service, and even now sets an example many of us would do well to copy.

The Mosquitos attracted many people to Warboys; one, a senior wing commander, badly wanted a piece of the act but could not adapt himself to flying by night. There was a glamour about the 'Mozzie' which drew them, but the prospect of lugging a 4,000-lb bomb to Berlin was not to everyone's taste. It was a young man's aeroplane demanding flexibility, rapid thought processes when the unforeseen happened and a high quality of airmanship. Cramped in the tiny cockpit, pilot and navigator, the long flights to far flung targets such as Berlin at high altitude required stamina. Flying at 30,000 feet, in darkness, the likelihood of interception was remote, whilst the heavy flak batteries could not reach them; thus casualties were rare. Accidents during training, usually fatal, were not unknown, however; an indication of the need to fly these aircraft with the greatest circumspection.

Loaded with a 4,000-lb bomb, the equivalent of the weight of bombs carried by the American Flying Fortress over the same distance, take-off could be tricky and on one occasion I witnessed a swing which resulted in the breakaway of the 'cookie' which rolled smoothly down the runway without exploding whilst the aircraft was wrecked; the crew escaping injury. The possession of a small but significant force of these speedy little aircraft enabled Bennett to continue to pound Berlin on those nights when bad weather ruled out the dispatch of the four-engined 'heavies'. The 'Mozzie', flying above the weather, needed nothing more than good base conditions for take-off and return.

My time at Warboys was short, and my posting to Sir Arthur Harris's headquarters near High Wycombe stemmed from the possession of a specialist qualification as a navigator. 'Spec Ns' were in short supply and, at that time, the label was held mainly by General Duties Officers – Flying Branch, which meant pilot trained officers such as myself. The navigators proper had come up with the war and would eventually take over – which was fair and reasonable – though it didn't happen without a struggle and some opposition from the old die-hards. The long pre-war Specialist Navigation course was almost entirely theory; few had opportunity to apply the mathematical solutions to the solving of the PZX triangle or the abstruse laws of conic sections, though as pilot-navigator on Atlantic Ferry duties I had earlier gained much from my time at the Navigation School. In the old days, the Coastal Command boys enjoyed a monopoly of sextant lore which they flaunted in the face of the RAF, but their time was past; the advent of radio and radar plus the disappearance of the flying-boat brought about their eclipse. The old 'Navigators'

Union', a select and haughty band of Coastal Command officers boasting salt-encrusted cap badges, disappeared into legend.

NOTES

1. Group Captain K.J. Rampling DSO, DFC was killed in a raid to Frankfurt on 22/23rd March 1944. Wing Commander J.F. Barron, DSO and Bar, DFC, DFM, was killed while acting as Master Bomber in a raid by a small force on the railway yards at Le Mans on 19/20th May 1944; the Deputy Master Bomber on that raid was also shot down. John Searby's friend, Wing Commander Guy Lockhart, DSO, DFC and Bar, was killed in an outstandingly successful raid on an important German tank gearbox factory at Friedrichshafen (on the Bodensee – Lake Constance, not Friedrichshafen-on-Rhine) on 27/28th April 1944. German officials later stated that this was the most damaging raid against their tank production in the whole war.

As Searby comments, these were savage casualties for 7 Squadron, with three highly experienced and much decorated squadron commanders being lost in two months. Little wonder that Searby counted himself fortunate to survive his own tour as squadron commander.

Ken Rampling and Guy Lockhart are both buried in Durnbach War Cemetery, which is in a beautiful setting in Bavaria, and Fraser Barron is buried in France.

2. See Note 1, at the end of Chapter 7 (page 148) for editor's comment on this affair. It is interesting that John Searby, who had served in both 5 and 8 Groups, sides completely with Bennett of 8 Group in his comments.

3. Wing Commander J.B. Tatnall, OBE, was killed when the 7 Squadron Lancaster in which he was flying as second pilot was shot down in the Berlin area on the night of 15/16th February 1944, the last but one raid in the Battle of Berlin. Severe damage was caused in Berlin that night but 43 heavy bombers were lost from the 875 on the raid.

The unlucky 7 Squadron lost four experienced crews that night (out of eighteen crews dispatched); only two men, one severely wounded, survived from the 30 men involved – just one example of Bomber Command's terrible casualties during the war.

CHAPTER TEN

Bomber Command HQ

In July 1944 I was posted to Bomber Command Headquarters to take up the appointment of Command Navigation Officer. I left Bennett with regret: he had been a good master and I respected his competence. He spoke our language and there was little formality. The exchange of the companionship of the 'sharp end' for the monastic confines of Command Headquarters was no great prospect, though I took pleasure in my immediate surroundings and a return to the beech-clad Chilterns after so many years. Leaving Princes Risborough, I drove through twisting lanes with the smell of new-mown hay borne on the wind, recalling excusions of an earlier day riding an ancient Douglas motor-cycle which I garaged secretly a few miles from Halton Camp. Stolen joys arc sweet – I broke the rules governing the riding of motor-cycles though it harmed nobody: a gallon of petrol cost a shilling and opened up a vast area of pleasure.

My first impression on entering the heavily guarded compound with its imposing iron gates was one of utter calm, broken only by the arrival of a staff car; the war and the bustle of the bomber airfields did not penetrate the green gloom resulting from the closely packed trees hiding the many buildings. Directed to the Air Staff block I found the office of the man I was to succeed and, though it was early afternoon, no ray of sunshine came through to dispel the semi-darkness of my future place of work.

I received a warm welcome, possibly stemming in part from the relief at seeing an end to his labours – his pleasure was almost indecent. He was off to take command of a bomber station and I was committed to a longish sojourn in a small office where the ceiling seemed to press on my shoulders. We were old friends, and I couldn't blame him; he had done his stint and was entitled to something.

The handover was brisk: 'You'll find everything you need to know in this filing cabinet – and the staff will fill you in with the rest.' After that, we embarked on a rapid tour of various offices and I was introduced as his relief. Everyone was friendly and wished me well.

The mess was comfortable though it bore a close resemblance to the inside of a cathedral, only the ushers were missing, whilst the massive grandfather clock in the hall with its distinctive chime put me in mind of Edgar Allan Poe. The walls of the dining room carried large pictures of former commanders-in-chief under whose stern scrutiny I took my first meal that evening. Next morning I started work, taking my place in the Ops Room where we awaited the arrival of the C-in-C to begin his morning conference.

From April to September 1944, Bomber Command was committed to the support of the Allied invasion of Europe. In the weeks preceding the launching of the vast armada of British and American divisions across the Channel, the work of preparation went ahead with the destruction of railway centres and airfields. This policy of interdiction was designed to isolate the beachheads and the immediate areas up to a 150 miles radius, cutting communications and denying the enemy the means of reinforcing his opposition to the landings. Sir Arthur Harris did nothing by halves and, having undertaken this role, he brought massive forces to bear before, during and after, the securing of a foothold on Hitler's Occupied Europe. Since all these targets lay within reach of the extremely accurate *Oboe* radar, they were attacked with a high degree of precision and devastating effect. In particular, the railway network suffered complete paralysis and, had it been otherwise, the enemy, operating on internal lines, could have moved his divisions swiftly to counter the threats to the Normandy beaches. In the event, the interdiction plan succeeded hugely and the aim was achieved.

Whereas Harris was convinced the heavy and constant bombing of the enemy's cities would bring about a capitulation, thus obviating the slaughter which he had witnessed in the First World War, he made a great contribution in a different fashion ... and the head-on clash with the enemy at full strength in Normandy was prevented. Rail, road and canal lines were blasted until the Germans could no longer bring up reinforcements and munitions with any degree of certainty that they would arrive and a point was reached where only small parties could move by night. Every request from the army commanders was met immediately if weather permitted and there were notable instances where packets of 200 Lancasters wiped out the dug-in tanks and artillery clearing the way ahead of our troops.

Apart from my main responsibilities in the co-ordination and improvement of navigation techniques, ably supported by the clever and energetic Nigel Bennett, my deputy, I took my turn down as Duty Group Captain in 'Hole', a commonly used term for the Command Operations Room lying sixty feet beneath the chalk of the Chiltern hillside. Here, with its vast spread of ancillary offices such as Intelligence and Photographic Interpretation, lay the heart of Bomber Command, where the daily planning took place following Harris's morning conference. Punctual to the minute he could be heard descending the stair, as we waited in an atmosphere of mild nervousness. His personality was powerful and he entered in a hushed silence, removing his hat and reaching into his breast pocket for his packet of American cigarettes and stuffing one into the holder he always used. The list of priority targets was handed to him by the senior Intelligence Officer and he would peruse it for a moment as we waited the outcome. Sir Robert Saundby, the Deputy Commander-in-Chief stood at his left hand with the Senior Air Staff Officer next to him and, after that, Air Commodore Ops and the rest of the staff in a half circle fronting his desk. It was a small drama, enacted every morning. Harris would make his choice and call for the weather chart. This was a matter for Doctor Spence, the Chief Met Officer, who spread out the synoptic chart and dilated on the prospects both for the target area and the home bases. Spence's task was no easy exercise: Harris had a feeling for weather and he probed thoroughly. Occasionally he would try to nudge the forecast in the direction he would have liked it to go but Spence, a mild and courteous individual, stood firm. Harris would smile faintly and give up: he enjoyed this kind of delving but he never overruled his Chief Met Officer: the responsibility for launching 1,000 heavy bombers was his alone and the provision of safe landing conditions for his crews was always on his mind.

The autumn and winter of 1944-45 occasionally produced serious problems, but Harris would never hazard his crews in fog and bad weather over this country. They might curse him for sending them out in appalling conditions over the North Sea and Germany but they had confidence in his landing the force back on the home bases or on safe diversionary airfields. Tired, battle-weary crews were vulnerable and at this point in the fortunes of Bomber Command not all possessed the experience and skill for getting back on the runway when the visibility was down to a hundred yards or less.

Once the preliminary decision as to the target and the size of the attacking force had been taken, Sir Arthur would leave for his own office and the staff got down to the details of routes, wave timing, diversionary attacks and similar matters. This first conference lasted but a few minutes; a second meeting with the C-in-C would take place at midday when all the loose ends had been tied up: in the meantime Saundby would consult with the commander of the Pathfinder Force as to the method of marking the aiming point and the use of Bennett's Mosquito force for making diversionary raids to fox the enemy as to the true target. Command Form 'A' would go out over the teleprinters, informing all who needed to know of the intentions of the Commander-in-Chief, to be followed later by a detailed Operation Order containing a mass of vital information; this was known as Command Form 'B' and would circulate to all groups.

Not every morning conference went smoothly; Sir Arthur would fire off questions at various members of his staff and it was no time for hesitation or half answers: he liked it straight. One morning I stood with the team awaiting our Commander-in-Chief, far from happy; a certain disquiet was evident stemming from the events of the previous night when a large force had been ordered to attack a Ruhr target. I had been on duty in the Ops Room with a member of the navigation staff preparing for the customary wind broadcasts. This involved averaging the wind speed and direction received by W/T from selected crews which was sent out as a broadcast to the force as a whole; thus, with every bomber applying the same wind values the force remained compact and the timing of the attack achieved greater accuracy. My colleague, the Duty Group Captain, had expressed his uneasiness about the way the weather for the return was shaping and the Duty Met Officer was called in for a further examination. Normally we would have informed the Deputy, Sir Robert Saundby, but he was absent and the Senior Air Staff Officer likewise.

The minutes ticked by to take off and we had a problem; the C-in-C disliked direct calls to his residence and it was unheard of for a mere group captain like me to cancel a full-blooded attack on an important target. Visibility at bases was reducing slowly and there was little time before several hundred heavy bombers left the ground with the likelihood of tricky conditions for getting back again. We chewed on the matter when, suddenly, my colleague picked up the green telephone and spoke to all group operations rooms throughout the command ... 'Operation cancelled with immediate effect.' It was done and there were white faces among the Ops Room staff. The order was irreversible and could not be changed. I looked at him and he shrugged his shoulders; if the fog failed to thicken, someone would be for the high jump on the morrow.

By nine o'clock we were all in our usual place in the Ops Room. Sir Robert Saundby and the others all knew the form and the weather at bases on the previous evening had not 'socked in' as expected, but had been marginal only. How would Sir Arthur react? We had not long to wait and he took his seat, lit up, and looked around ... then the usual question:

'How did we get on last night?'

Silence; and the C-in-C looked around enquiringly, impatient for an answer.

Saundby spoke,

'The operation was called off, sir.' Somewhat puzzled, Harris waited for more information and Sir Robert was distinctly uneasy.

'Who cancelled it?' and my colleague, unable to bear the strain any longer suddenly burst out:

'I did, sir.'

Another pause, then: 'Why?' and the answer came swiftly: 'I was not satisfied we could get them back; the fog was closing in.'

A grunt from Harris and that was all; the bomb I had expected did not burst.

After the early conference we did not see Harris again: Saundby dealt with the review at midday. If a later question arose he disappeared into the C-in-C's office next door and emerged with the answer. Sir Arthur remained remote and Sir Robert settled all day to day matters. It was rare for heads of branches to be called into the Chief's sanctum, but it happened to me after an incident at the time the enemy was breaking out of the Falaise Gap where the Lancasters were directed to bomb German armour. As a safety measure our bombers dropped on a timed run by radar in order to avoid accidents with our own troops, and a mistake occurred with unfortunate results. The responsible squadron commanders were sacked within the hour. One was from overseas and his government's representative in London arrived at Command

Headquarters to protest. A call from Peggy Wherry, the WAAF in charge of his secretariat, and armed with the relevant *Gee* chart, I was ushered inside where an air marshal in a dark blue uniform sat beside the C-in-C's desk. Harris looked up as I entered,

'Have you got what I want?'

'Yes, sir.'

He nodded toward his visitor. 'Show him what happened.'

I spread out the chart and explained the reason for the precise timed run to the objective but I did not finish before Harris interrupted, asking his visitor if he had heard enough. The air marshal nodded: Harris looked at me and said abruptly, 'Get out.' I rolled up the chart and left quickly; the atmosphere was thunderous. A few minutes later looking out of my window I observed the visitor emerge from the front door of the Air Staff Block and climb into his car. What happened I never knew but it seemed Harris's action had been challenged and he was not a man to brook interference from outside his command.

Although the Pathfinder Force, initially resisted by Harris, had been going for two years by the time I arrived at Command Headquarters and, in the opinion of the majority had more than justified itself, there was still a backwash swilling gently to and fro. On my first meeting with 'Daddy' Dawes, Senior Personnel Officer, he was less than polite about Bennett and a few days later, when I made a courtesy call on the Air Officer in charge of Training – AOT – he referred to my late master as a mountebank; a remark deeply resented.

I knew nothing of Bomber Command 'politics'; before going to High Wycombe my association with high ranking officers had been rare enough, so that I was surprised and sometimes angered by snide remarks from individuals who should have known better. The fact that I wore a Pathfinder Badge did not please some, I was to discover, but in time I lived it down. Much later in the day, when I became aware of all the wrangling which had taken place before the Air Ministry in the person of the Chief of the Air Staff had forced the decision to form Pathfinder Force on Sir Arthur Harris, I began to understand. I never heard Harris criticise the work of the Pathfinders and certainly not Sir Robert Saundby who was the fairest of men and one whom it was a pleasure to serve. That cool winds should blow in the corridors of power I had yet to learn.

At this stage of the war the Navigation and Signals Branches were closely linked by virtue of the increasing use of radar and other aids. The signallers installed and maintained the intricate electronic devices developed by the scientists for the improvement of track keeping and target location and it is safe to say that Bomber Command stood or fell by the quality of its signals staff. Bomber Command drew some of the best officers of that day in the body of specialists which comprised the staff of Air Commodore Dalton-Morris. Liaison was satisfactory between the branches and our opposite numbers spared no effort to smooth the path of the navigator out in the front line. Out on the bomber stations, the numbers of maintenance personnel responsible for electronics had swollen greatly since the days when the Whitleys and Wellingtons carried nothing more than a wireless transmitter and a short range voice communication set known as the TR9 plus the crew intercom equipment. *Gee*, H_2S, *Monica* and other black boxes called for daily maintenance and a hefty supply of radar mechanics to keep them serviceable – a source of constant worry to the Chief Signals Officer; and the situation was growing almost daily. Thus, when Dalton-Morris spoke to me one day about the problems of servicing a thousand H_2S sets every morning, I listened sympathetically, though it was none of my business and I could make no suggestions that might help. I was concerned only with the operation of the equipment, whether it worked or it didn't.

Maintaining contact with the group staffs was important; they often came up with suggestions which could benefit the command as a whole; 'group thinking' was jealously guarded, however, and one needed to be cautious: the 'Bomber Barons' exercised complete autonomy over their stations and squadrons, and visiting firemen tended to be suspect. My favourite 'Baron' was Roddy Carr, Air Officer Commanding No 4 Bomber Group operating Halifaxes, an officer much respected who had borne the heat and burden of the day almost from the beginning of the bomber offensive. Powerfully built, he was almost the archetype English gentleman though born in New Zealand, with an easy manner and the gift of putting one completely at ease in his presence. He had a good word for the Pathfinder Force and expressed admiration for its commander, who had served under him. He wished me well in my new job and gave me carte blanche to visit his stations, making me thoroughly comfortable and displaying a real concern for the improvement of our navigation techniques. Whereas his opposite numbers in Nos 1 and No 5 Groups were reckoned both 'Harris men', whose association with our commander-in-chief stemmed from pre-war days, Air Vice-Marshal Carr seemed to retain his own individuality, pursuing an even path without becoming involved in any kind of controversy. He gets no mention in Harris's own account of the bomber offensive, though by virtue of his nigh-on four year stint in command of an important slice of Harris's force, one might expect some acknowledgement. He must have been good at his job to have retained command of his group for the whole of the time Harris was Commander-in-Chief. Lumped with the Halifax, which was inferior to the Lancaster, it was not his good fortune to have been associated with any single outstanding attack, though in gallantry and sheer guts the Halifax crews were second to none, producing such outstanding leaders as Tait, Cheshire, Robinson, Iveson and Marks – all flight lieutenants or flight commanders at one time in No 4 Group. Like master – like man ... one encountered nothing but friendliness on stations and squadrons; Carr's straightforwardness and lack of pomposity was reflected in his subordinates ... visiting staff officers from HQBC were not always popular but in No 4 Group it was a pleasure to do business.

Our own headquarters was not a cheerful place; at least that was my reaction. Sir Arthur Harris was a remote figure and, apart from his morning conference, he was seldom seen again, save when he got into his Bentley to go home. Heads of branches were called to the sanctum but in the main all day-to-day business was executed by the Deputy C-in-C, Sir Robert Saundby. Admittedly, Sir Arthur bore a heavy burden and a great deal of time was taken up with policy: he was frequently at odds with the Air Staff in Whitehall over priorities and waged a constant battle with the Ministry of Economic Warfare and similar bodies. He bore total responsibility for the direction of the bomber offensive and fought a set-piece battle five nights in each week, on average. The strain must have been considerable and might well have broken a lesser man. He did not visit his squadrons, save on very rare occasions, so that it is all the more remarkable that his personality should have reached into every crew room throughout his vast command. At the time of Bomber Command's greatest trial, in the winter of 1943-44, when the crews slogged their way to 'the Big City' through storm and icing conditions, incurring severe casualties, he was a factor for morale! It is perfectly true; men took pride in repeated sorties, facing a vengeful Luftwaffe, too often terminating in a hopeless search for what lay beneath layer upon layer of dense cloud – Berlin. For some, Harris was a kind of symbol for air warfare at its cruellest extension, knowing with near-certainty that their number would come up sooner or later, and not unlike the slaughter at the Somme and Ypres 25 years earlier. Nineteen, 20 and 21 years of age, a dozen operations made them veterans, though a high proportion never reached this stage; many were cut down by cannon fire on their first or second sortie – yet morale was not broken when the end came on 24th and 30th of March 1944 over Berlin and Nuremberg, with losses totalling 166 four-engined bombers, each carrying a crew of seven or eight officers and NCOs. 'Dented' is the right word.

Standing in the little half circle of staff officers at Harris's morning conference, when he was informed of the casualties from the previous night's operations, I sometimes wondered what thought he gave to them when he returned to the quiet of his own office. In the Operations Room they were numbers only, necessary subtractions from the day's muster – not individuals; it seemed we were all too far away from the terrifying aspect of death by night over the enemy's country or the ditching in the North Sea. Out on the windy airfields of Yorkshire and Lincolnshire casualties meant people – gaps in the flight commander's Battle Order – whereas in the solemn calm of the Headquarters Operations Room they could never be more than just numbers, deeply regretted, but not personal. For those whose link with the sharp end was still strong – having recently been engaged in active operations over Germany – the loss of friends was keenly felt but for others whose whole war had been a matter of staff routine there could be little sense of involvement. It was only long after the war ended that I became aware of Harris's deep concern.

That autumn, on 19th September 1944, Guy Gibson was killed after an attack on München Gladbach, the day after my visit to him at Coningsby. I found him little changed and not very enthusiastic over his current appointment as a member of the Base Commander's staff. He was itching to get back to full flying duties and after lunch took me into one of the hangars to see a Mosquito, saying he intended to use this aircraft when doing the odd sortie. Something of the old spirit was evident as he talked and the time passed happily. He saw me off in the little Proctor, waved goodbye and that was the last I was to see of him. A great leader was lost in Guy Gibson. Of all the war-time airmen, he stands out best; perhaps it was his boyishness – his liking for fun and having his men around him – and humanity ... he smoothed the exit of an officer older than he, who lacked the guts to fly; and whereas a lesser man might have made a fuss, and flung the book at him, Guy said, 'Well – he's not bad really; he's a square peg in a round hole and it's not his fault he can't face up to it. I'll fix it with the medics.'

One day I was in the Public Relations office where I was shown a draft of Guy's book *Enemy Coast Ahead*. How or why they had it there I do not know, but they were all journalists ... John Lawrence, Hugh Massingham, Clutton-Brock and sometimes Richard Dimbleby who was an accredited war correspondent for the BBC. I had seen part of it before and this caused surprise until I related how Guy had written much of it at Syerston ... in a blue school exercise book. The function of the Relations officers was one of publicising the work of Bomber Command and a few minutes spent in their company was a mighty relief from all that went on downstairs. The wit flew back and forth; nothing was sacred ... Air marshals did not count for much in their world – but a first hand account of what went on in the squadrons and stations merited instant attention. All very worthwhile people and very generous with their cups of tea – of which there was no limit. It helped the job along. Hugh Massingham was a favourite: six feet plus and powerfully built he excelled in gentleness.

Dimbleby was a popular figure. Boyish, with a good sense of the ridiculous, he was invariably dressed in a khaki battledress – somewhat travel stained – wearing an army officers' cap, bearing little resemblance to the dignified and polished individual who later conducted the weekly *Panorama* television show. He took me to lunch one day at Simpson's in the Strand after a conducted tour of the BBC, where a dozen people came over to our table to greet him. Despite his rise to fame as a broadcaster he played it all down and told some fascinating stories of his time with the Eighth Army in North Africa and his two weeks at sea in one of HM submarines. He had great sympathy for the aircrew of Bomber Command and confessed that his ride with Gibson over Berlin was less than comfortable. One of his greatest disappointments was missing the final *Tirpitz* attack which took place on 12th November 1944. This was a remarkable feat of precision bombing by Nos 617 and 9 Squadrons involving a 1,000-mile flight to the target and another 1,000 back to base – and not a man was lost in the operation! Strike photos displayed in the Operations Room the day following the attack created immense interest: the constant threat imposed by the existence of this powerful warship had been removed,to the great satisfaction of the Royal Navy. Her sister ship, *Bismarck*, had been sunk in 1941 at great cost in a surface action involving the loss of the *Hood* from which only three of her complement of fourteen hundred officers and men were saved. *Primus inter pares*, Willie Tait must surely rank as the greatest bomber captain of all time; self effacing, incredibly modest he fought his war from the earliest beginning right to the bitter end, tightlipped about his own achievements and avoiding publicity.

Harris never entered the mess during the time I spent at Bomber Command Headquarters, though his deputy, Sir Robert Saundby, was present in the Blue Room every evening. He would stay for an hour mixing easily with officers of all ranks discoursing on a variety of subjects from fly-fishing to model railways. He filled the gap between Harris and the staff. Like all true 'greats' he had the gift for putting one at ease so that he was a very popular visitor. A keen naturalist, he sometimes was seen in the mess gardens in the late evening armed with a butterfly net and a jam jar – catching moths for his collection; and he was handy with a pencil. His 'doodles' – usually left behind after chairing one of the many conferences which took place in the course of a week were eagerly gathered up – superb little drawings of butterflies and other insects. He was the perfect foil for Sir Arthur, whom he served loyally, yet was content to remain in the background: thus, he was the recipient of all grumbles and complaints from the group commanders who deemed it safer to try it on Sir Robert in the first instance! He was, it seemed, Harris's 'Marshal Berthier', zealous for the reputation of the Command and untiring in his efforts to ensure that nothing was left undone which ought to be done.

During the period in which Bomber Command came under Eisenhower, Harris was less than happy about the lull afforded to German industry and the de-housing of the population of the cities. In particular, the continued bombing of the rocket sites across the Channel he regarded as a waste of time and bombs but it was not until mid-September that the shackles were removed.

Even so, there were many requests from the Army for support; all of which received the best possible treatment though our Commander-in-Chief sometimes blew his top when asked to lay on packets of Lancasters to silence German batteries. At the crossing of the Rhine at Wesel the effectiveness of accurate bombing by two hundred of these aircraft was such that only a handful of casualties resulted among the soldiers; without such support, the dug-in German tanks and guns would have held up the advance for days – with the loss of hundreds of our men. Monty's signal of appreciation to Harris was seen in the Ops Room and our master derived satisfaction therefrom. Always at the back of his mind lay the slaughter of the 1914-18 War and whatever might be done to alleviate the task of the soldiers was tackled with energy and dispatch. He may have grumbled occasionally but the response for assistance was both adequate and immediate.

One day in March I was asked by John Lawrence – press relations – to take him to Paris in one of the Communication Flight aircraft. It was my day off from the Ops Room and there was little doing in the office so I agreed and set off from Halton in an Oxford trainer. This was my first view of France in daylight and, after crossing from Dungeness to Cap Gris Nez, we flew over a countryside ravaged by the fighting and marked with thousands upon thousands of bomb craters. The destruction was fearful, continuing all the way to Paris where we landed at Le Bourget. The airfield and hangars had been shelled and only a single clear path contrived for take-off and landing. As we drove into the city there was a deadness about everything and few people were seen – a ghost town it appeared until we approached the centre and the area around the Arc de Triomphe. The Place de la Concorde was full of American lorries and parked guns with American soldiers lying full length asleep on the pavements and on almost any flat surface where they could stretch out.

The stonework and parapets of the bridge were pitted by bullets and the general scene was depressing: few people moved about the streets and no civilian motor vehicles were observed. We lunched at the Officers' Club – formerly the Rothschild town house and a very beautiful building. Here all was different – smartly dressed women squired by uniformed officers – snow white table cloths – flowers everywhere and an atmosphere of gaiety overall. Yet outside, Paris was starving – literally. I took particular note of the smart hats worn by the women and some were quite remarkable; it seemed that the turban was back in fashion and one woman wore a tall conical hat of intricate pattern. A new vogue perhaps? Our guide soon explained, certainly the turban was popular – it had swept Paris over the recent weeks following the liberation. Why the turban? Well, as you see it hides the hair completely – and some ladies have suffered the misfortune of having their hair cut short! *Pourquoi, monsieur?* A slight hesitation and we got the truth; any woman suspected of co-habitating with the enemy lost her crowning glory; an infuriated mob removed it as a punishment! Including some innocent victims, at whom the finger had been pointed.

On the return I flew into bad weather with a strong headwind. It was getting dark when I crossed the Channel and after searching in poor visibility for a suitable airfield I put down at Lympne, much to the relief of John Lawrence who lost no time in ordering a car to get him to London. I think he had suffered a bad quarter of an hour before I eventually found Lympne, and hurried his departure lest I filled up and pressed on in the dark. I assured him I had no intention of so doing but he had had enough and made quite certain he flew no more that day, or night. From Lympne I was taken to Hawkinge where I spent the night, returning next morning early to Halton and Command Headquarters. When he arrived at the Public Relations office next morning I was already in my own and he assumed I had made it in the dark. He never asked me again to fly him anywhere. He was a thoroughly nice man with a great reputation as a journalist and subsequently produced a very fine book on No 5 Bomber Group and 617 Squadron whom he held in high regard.

The lobby against bombing of German cities had gathered momentum since the summer and criticism of Harris was beginning to spread. The Church was well represented in the persons of bishops whilst eminent Labour politicians made their views known. Harris was unmoved and went so far as to consent to an address to his staff from Sir Stafford Cripps, though the purpose of this talk was by no means clear. This lecture was entitled 'Christianity and the Bomber'; I was present and, whilst we heard a lot about God, we got nothing about the bomber! Harris attended and sat on the platform, out of deference to a Cabinet Minister, his face devoid of expression, as Cripps bumbled through sheet after sheet of notes and when it was all over we left wondering what it was all about.

To this day I have no clear recollection of a single word he said and my diary contains the simple phrase: 'Stafford Cripps lecture was all Christianity and no bomber – we were sold a pup.'

That, ultimately, the name of our Commander-in-Chief would be besmirched by lesser men and the crews of Bomber Command be denied the campaign medal which was their right still sends a shock wave through most of us. Much as I disliked Harris's brusqueness and his apparent insensitivity, he was without question one of our greatest commanders. The fact that he kept his mouth tightly shut and did not attempt to refute the charges brought against him by mere pygmies is to his everlasting credit. But, then, they were not worthy of his steel!

The strategic bomber created a new dimension in war. Whereas for the Navy and Army who pursued a well-beaten path marked by battle honours, and loaded with tradition, the Second World War was a continuation of the First. The Royal Navy followed policies and methods, time honoured and familiar, from the very beginning; likewise the Army went into France in 1939 much as it had done a generation earlier, but the Royal Air Force embarked on a period of trial and error with no clearly defined role save that of defending this country from air attack. In this it succeeded nobly: Fighter Command won its place in history over a period of a few months. Bomber Command, ill-equipped with antiquated aircraft, provided the only means of carrying the offensive into the German homeland. There were no guide lines and in the first phase our attacks were often ineffective though the morale of the British public was greatly strengthened thereby. Harris assumed command at a time when better aircraft and new devices for finding the objectives were promised but these alone could not have shaped the force into the weapon of massive destruction which ultimately destroyed German industry. Only a man of Harris's quality, possessing his rugged strength and firm belief in his powers as a commander, could have created such a weapon. Frequently, his ideas and actions ran counter to those held by the Air Staff in Whitehall – but there are precedents. Harris abhorred place seekers, bureaucrats and 'yes men' who wished to placate an enemy so vile as were the Nazis. Alas, he fell victim to the Stracheys and the Attlees – the bishops and others – who conveniently forgot the murder of seven million Jews and the enslavement of Occupied Europe. The sacrifice of 55,000 airmen of Bomber Command was not to be honoured by a campaign medal – though any NAAFI manager serving more than 48 hours in Italy was accorded a similar honour!

I was present on the morning Dresden was selected for attack. The initiative came from Whitehall and not from Sir Arthur. Winston Churchill had pressed the Secretary of State for Air as to what plans he had to harry the German retreat from Breslau and the Chief of the Air Staff, Sir Charles Portal, came up with the bombing of Dresden, Leipzig and Chemnitz ... and, 'any other cities where a severe blitz will not only cause confusion in the evacuation from the East but will also hamper the movement of troops from the West.' The executive order came from Sir Norman Bottomley, Deputy Chief of the Air Staff, in which Harris was told to get on with it ... which he did on 13th February. The Americans followed up this night attack in force the next day and on two further occasions utterly wrecking what was left after Bomber Command had finished. That Sir Arthur should carry the full responsibility is grossly unfair, yet that is what happened.

With the end of the war not far off, I left Bomber Command for pastures new. Sir Ralph Cochrane had taken over the rapidly expanding Transport Command and he asked for me to be posted to his staff at Bushey Park. This was a fortunate move since Bomber Command was grinding to a halt whilst Transport Command was coming to the fore: a vast amount of work lay ahead, setting up a world-wide network of communications; the scope was limitless. The whole world was on the move it seemed ... but that is another story. I left Bomber Command with regret and, ultimately, I would return but it was a wrench; too much of my life was bound up in the squadrons and airfields from which the bombers had been launched; too many of my friends had not returned. The bomber offensive cost us 55,000 lives of which more than 47,000 were lost in action – many of whom have no known grave. More than 4,000 were wounded in action and ten thousand were taken prisoner; a further 4,000 suffered wounds and disablement whilst engaged in non-operational duties which involved training others to fly the bombers. Yet we have no campaign medal!

This slight on men who carried the war into the enemy's country continuously over five long years will remain to the end of time. '*Per ardua ad astra*'. There could be no more fitting motto. It was a matter of '*Per ardua.*' from start to finish. From the December of 1939, when the Wellingtons suffered 50 per cent casualties on two of the three attacks on the enemy's fleet, through the agonising period of the Battle of Berlin terminating in the loss of more than 90 four-engined bombers over Nuremberg, each crewed by seven or eight officers and NCOs whose courage and devotion to duty was never lacking. The merest sergeant pilot, captaining a Lancaster or Halifax, briefed to fly for six or seven hours, and much of it over enemy territory, flogged his way in all weathers out and back, if he was so fortunate with none to hold his hand, and with six men behind him entirely dependent upon his skill and judgement; through the hell of the heavy flak and frequently hunted by fighters. when the pressure was on he would be called upon three and four nights in each week. If he was unlucky then 'Failed to return' was his only epitaph – neatly written against his name in the squadron record book – and another would step into the breach. In our letters to next-of-kin we would express our deep regret that a son or brother should have been lost and saying, with great sincerity, 'he will be missed'. Indeed, he *was* 'missed' for a time – but, inevitably, the monstrous pressure of events quickly swallowed him. One endeavoured, in each of these painful letters to include some personal touch, however small, but it was not always easy. Toward the end of the battle for the enemy's capital, crews came and went without having really belonged to the squadron. They came off the transport from the Conversion Unit and a day or two later they were posted as 'missing'.

'I want my aircraft flown to the limit, and I expect flight and squadron commanders to set an example.' The words of Air Marshal Alec Coryton, then in command of No 5 Bomber Group, when he interviewed me in September 1942 for the post of flight commander. Most squadron commanders of his group at that time were a by-word for guts and determination: he was well served. Flight commanders were readily expendable and the casualty lists back up these words. There were no time-serving DSOs dished out in Coryton's day. When I moved to the Pathfinder Force a similar situation obtained; Bennett had no use for commanders who failed to come up to scratch! I quote from his book *Pathfinder*:

This battle (Berlin) was indeed the bitterest part of the war for me, for not only was it gravely important we should succeed and thereby confirm the effects of Hamburg, but also it was bitter because of the great losses which we suffered … I lost a number of squadron commanders and senior flight commanders, and at one stage I thought that the backbone of the Pathfinder Force was broken.

Marks, Fraser-Barron, Hilton, Rampling, Robinson, Abercromby, Cousens, Lockhart, and the list is by no means complete ... all dedicated leaders in command of Pathfinder squadrons whilst the list of flight commanders is impressive.

After many years, stories grow in the telling and, whilst it is inevitable that all were not cast in the same mould, Bomber Command stood or fell by the quality of the men who filled the post of squadron and flight commander. The distinction achieved by commanders such as Gibson, Cheshire and Tait reflected more than isolated instances of gallantry; each possessed a long record of operational duty. Pickard, Fauquier, Ralston, combining painstaking thoroughness with personal bravery, were an inspiration to the men they led ... and there were, among the several bomber groups, many such commanders who, if they did not hit the headlines, contributed massively to the success of the bomber offensive. If we go back to the beginning we find them present in the persons of Kellett and Griffiths, each leading formations against almost impossible odds in determined efforts to find and bomb Wilhelmshaven. If there were over-ripe apples in our particular barrel, as hinted by one writer, then I did not encounter them.

Bomber Command entered the war quite unprepared for the task before it and deficient in nearly everything except the spirit of its crews ... The penalty of unpreparedness was a severe and a prolonged one. The aircraft had not the means of defending themselves ... nor of finding and hitting their targets with anything like the expected degree of precision in darkness.

This extract is taken from the Official History of the Bombing Offensive against Germany and, to those of us who served in the newly formed Bomber Command, it recalls a period of change and re-organisation calculated to switch the role of the Royal Air Force from one of policing our Empire overseas to one of confronting the threat from a potential enemy within striking distance of these islands.

When the balloon went up, our Navy and Army took up from where they had left off in 1919: their roles were clearly defined but, apart from the need to defend this island against air attack, the Royal Air Force had to carve out new policies, without the benefit of anything more than the achievements of the Royal Flying Corps a generation earlier. The Independent Air Force of 1918 came too late in the day to leave guide lines for those who came after and the plans made in the late thirties for intervention bombing of Germany rested on daylight attack: without long range escort fighters such plans were impracticable. The 'blanket of the dark' was resorted to after the disasters in the Heligoland Bight in December 1939: yet we had neither the training nor the means of discovering and bombing our objectives. It was from these roots that Harris's command sprang; yet to the bitter end we lacked the means of defending ourselves: the miserable pea-shooters in the bomber turrets left us virtually helpless whilst the escort fighter, sorely needed by night after 1943, never got off the drawing board. In his excellent book *The Guns of the Royal Air Force* Mr G.F. Wallace makes this statement:

> At higher levels the advice of the service was sometimes disregarded by the politicians, often with disastrous results. In the gunnery field an obvious example was Lord Beaverbrook's decision to stop work on the development of the Hispano 20-mm gun turret which left our bombers without effective defence during their operations over Germany later in the war.*

Towards the end of the war we did indeed fit a 5-inch turret into the Lancasters of No 1 Group: Harris had fought long and bitterly for this and enlisted the services of Alf Rose – a patriotic gentleman and head of Rose Bros of Gainsborough who tackled the problem with enthusiasm: 'They produced a first class turret of revolutionary design equipped with 5-inch guns ... in less than a year ... and, of course, we should never have got it if we had not ordered it on our own and in an entirely irregular way.' Had the 5-inch turret been fitted to all heavy bombers from the beginning our casualties might well have been halved. Harris fought bureaucracy with might and main: from the battles in the Heligoland Bight onwards the uselessness of the .303-inch turret guns was readily apparent but nothing would move the Ministry of

* William Kimber, 1972.

Aircraft Production to take instant urgent action to remedy this situation. Like the Army in 1914, where the establishment allowed for two machine guns per battalion, the aircrew of Bomber Command faced the murderous fire of the enemy's 20-mm cannon with rifle calibre bullets. Forty years on this is still a matter for bitter debate among the survivors.

More than forty years after the events related in the foregoing pages, the journal I kept for each of the five years of war reads like ancient history; and the gulf grows wider with each year that passes. Much of the content is raw and jerkily written, though starkly correct in time and circumstance: names are there to which I can readily put faces – ghosts who greet me – fresh as the day I last saw them in the pride of their youth. The best I have known are sealed in these pages. I wrote with scrupulous honesty, often in haste, as if time was not on my side. It could not be otherwise. It had been said that 'war is largely a business of waiting' but that did not apply to the bomber crews – there were no long intervals between set-piece battles – only the sordid, repetitive forays over the enemy's country, night after night when it was very cold, very noisy and very uncomfortable – scared stiff much of time and thankful to see the familiar flare-path on the home airfield after six, seven or eight hours.

Epilogue

The Little People who inhabit the hill had always been there. They saw the westward march of Vespasian's Second Legion and the storming of Maiden Castle, having warned the proud Roman he would have no easy task. The Britons are stubborn, they told him, and value freedom more than life itself; and so it proved. A thousand years later they encouraged Harold in his march south after the battle of Stamford Bridge to Senlac Hill where his House Carles defended the Standard until all were slain. Sad at the death of their hero they went underground and were heard of no more until Halton Camp was built for the young men of the Royal Flying Corps who fought so bravely on the Western Front in France. By then the Little People had come back to the hill overlooking the Vale of Aylesbury and were often heard by those who took the trouble to make the climb and walk in the cool beechwoods. When England was threatened with invasion a generation later, they rejoiced over the victory won in the Battle of Britain and the Long Beards went around saying, 'I told you so – these young men are worthy of their forebears.'

Personal Postscript

by Diana Searby

Without Martin Middlebrook's help, this book would not have been published. I thank him for his detailed research work. Many of John's friends perished and their graves are scattered across Europe. Through pilgrimages led by Mr Middlebrook to battlefields and war cemeteries, these warriors are not forgotten.

In John's memory, thank you, Martin.

John Searby's Operational Record

With 405 (Canadian) Squadron, 4 Group:

31.10.1941	Hamburg
7.11.1941	Boulogne

With 106 Squadron, 5 Group:

6.11.1942	Genoa
13.11.1942	Genoa
18.11.1942	Turin
20.11.1942	Turin
22.11.1942	Stuttgart
6.12.1942	Mannheim
8.12.1942	Turin
21.12.1942	Munich
13.1.1943	Essen, aircraft damaged by flak
16.1.1943	Berlin
27.1.1943	Düsseldorf
13.2.1943	Lorient
14.2.1943	Milan
21.2.1943	Bremen
25.2.1943	Nuremberg
26.2.1943	Cologne
28.2.1943	St Nazaire
1.3.1943	Berlin
5.3.1943	Essen
8.3.1943	Nuremberg
9.3.1943	Munich
11.3.1943	Stuttgart
12.3.1943	Essen
4.4.1943	Kiel
4.5.1943	Dortmund

With 83 Squadron, 8 (Pathfinder Force) Group:

23.5.1943	Dortmund
29.5.1943	Wuppertal
19.6.1943	Montchanin
12.7.1943	Turin, Master Bomber trial
24.7.1943	Hamburg, aircraft damaged by collision on return
14.8.1943	Milan
17.8.1943	Peenemünde, Master Bomber
6.9.1943	Munich
16.9.1943	Modane
3.10.1943	Kassel

Total: 37 operational flights, dropping approximately 170 tons of bombs on 24 raids to Germany, 8 to Italy and 5 to France; all operations were completed.

Index